The Dido Papers

The Letters of a Victorian Midshipman

John Johnson-Allen

Whittles Publishing, an imprint of Porto Press
3 Connaught Road
St Albans AL3 5RX, UK

www.whittlespublishing.com

© 2025 John Johnson-Allen
ISBN 978-184995-603-1

Also by
John Johnson-Allen

They Were Just Skulls:
The Naval Career of Fred Henley, Last Survivor of HM Submarine Truculent
ISBN 978-184995-404-4

'Rosy' Wemyss, Admiral of the Fleet:
The Man Who Created Armistice Day
ISBN 978-184995-485-3

Printed and bound by CPI Group (UK) Ltd, Croydon, CR0 4YY

Contents

Acknowledgements

For their assistance I would like to thank:

- The Master and Fellows of Churchill College, Cambridge, for their permission to reproduce extracts and illustrations from the Archive of the Papers of Sir Bryan Godfrey-Faussett.

- Ian Killick and Ann-Marie Fitzsimmons of the Archive Department of the United Kingdom Hydrographic Office, Taunton, for their warm welcome and enthusiastic assistance in sourcing contemporary Admiralty Pilots and charts. Extracts from those charts have been used with the consent of the Hydrographic Office.

- The staff of Churchill College Archive Centre for their help and assistance in sourcing the necessary material from Bryan Godfrey-Faussett's very large archive.

- Again, Keith Whittles and his team for their skill in turning my manuscript into the book you have in front of you.

- Caroline Petherick, editor without equal, for both her wicked sense of humour and for her assistance in polishing my work to its final state.

- And of course, last but not least, my wife Claire for her support and forbearance whilst, once more, my mind was distracted. I could not do it without her.

Glossary of naval terms

Brig: a two-masted vessel, carrying square sails on each mast

Bulwarks: raised sides at the edge of the deck

Cutter: a ship's boat, propelled by oars or by sail

Dirk: a small sword worn by midshipmen

Gunroom: midshipmen's accommodation

Knot (abbr. kn): unit of speed; 1 knot is 1 nautical mile per hour

Krooman/men: members of the Kroo tribe, famous for their seamanship and maritime skills

Main top: platform on the mainmast about a quarter of the way up, at the junction of the lower part of the mainmast and the upper sections of the mainmast, ie topmast, t'gallant and royal. (Easily confused with the crow's nest, at the top of the mast.)

Make fast: secure a vessel to a fixed point, to another vessel or to the land

Masts: When a ship has only one mast it is always called the mainmast. If there are two masts their names are determined by their size and position: if the foremost mast is the larger it is called the mainmast and the other is called the mizzenmast; where there are more than two masts they are called fore, main and mizzen; if there is a fourth mast the aftermost is the jigger mast. (*Admiralty Manual of Seamanship*)

Midship: the middle part of the ship (BBGF's abbreviation: mid = midshipman)

Pinnace: a ship's boat, larger than a cutter, and similarly powered

Ram bow: a type of ship's bow which projects forwards under water, to ram and disable an enemy ship

Royal sail: normally the uppermost sail on the mast of a square-rigged ship

Ship ribbons: worn on crew's hats, and embroidered with the ship's name

Topgallant sail: an upper sail, hung from the topgallant mast; the third-highest sail

Wardroom: the officers' accommodation

Yardarms/yards: in a square-rigged ship, horizontal spars hung from the masts, from which the sails are suspended

Author's note

As these letters were written in the late 19th century, some of the views expressed in them and words used are no longer acceptable. As, however, they are contemporary to that time I have retained most of them to retain the reality of the period.

There are, however, many instances of a specific word that is now unprintably offensive – though not intended so at the time – that could be transcribed as 'n****s'. As this in itself, however, would attract attention, I have, despite the risk of some readers feeling uncomfortable even so, replaced it with the less inflammatory 'natives' throughout.

As far as ships are concerned, although these days they have lost their femininity, becoming a mere 'it', I have retained their female gender not only in Godfrey-Faussett's writing, but in my own as well.

Next, while this is a faithful transcription of the words in BBGF's letters, I have in some places inserted a modicum of punctuation and paragraphing, and have very occasionally inserted a word of my own in [square brackets] per publishing convention, in order for a reader who is not the intended recipient of those letters to grasp their meaning more swiftly and easily.

Next, where I have been unable to decipher a word or phrase, I have indicated this with 'xxxxx'; and an ellipsis, … , shows where text has been omitted.

Finally, I have changed ship names and words originally underlined for emphasis into italics, again per publishing convention.

Foreword

The invitation to write the foreword to this book arose out of a casual conversation I'd had with John Johnson-Allen on the margins of a meeting held recently in London.

He and I are old friends, and share a common interest in maritime matters and literature. Over the years I have enjoyed reading his books, and I asked what he was planning to write about next. He brought me up to date and said he had just finished writing one about a naval officer called Captain Sir Bryan Godfrey-Faussett whose diaries, journals and letters from his time at sea in the early years of his career in the Victorian era had provided a rich source of material for a book. He added that he thought it highly unlikely I had ever heard of him.

By an astonishing coincidence, however, the name *did* mean something to me, and I ventured to ask if by any chance this Captain Godfrey-Faussett had a son whose nickname was 'Feather'. Although John didn't know that, what he did know was that there had been two sons, that the younger one had been a pilot in the Fleet Air Arm during the war, and that he had played a part in the sinking of the *Bismarck* on 26 May 1941.

'You aren't going to believe this,' I replied, 'but your book is about the father of that Fleet Air Arm pilot. He served in 810 Naval Air Squadron flying Swordfish aircraft from HMS *Ark Royal* between March 1940 and July 1941. And my father was his observer throughout that time – though not, as it happens, during the attack on the *Bismarck*.'

Some six weeks after the *Bismarck* encounter my father was reappointed and returned to the United Kingdom as a watchkeeper in another ship. He had hoped to be back home in Scotland in time for the birth of his first-born child in mid-July 1941, but in the event he missed the birth, in Edinburgh, by two days. I happened to be the new baby boy.

I was baptised four weeks later in the kirk of Southdean, a tiny village set deep in the Scottish borders overlooking the Cheviot Hills. In addition to the minister and myself, only five people were present. Missing from the gathering was my godfather, but the family records reveal that his name was Lieutenant David Godfrey-Faussett DSC Royal Navy, and that he had given me £5 and a Harrods Bank money box as a christening present.

I never knowingly met my godfather, and it wasn't until I was much older that I learned he had been killed while flying at night from HMS *Condor*, the Royal Naval Air Station at Arbroath, in March 1942. He was 28. It so happened that my father was also

L–R: John Lang (my father), the observer, and David Godfrey-Faussett, the pilot.
By permission, Lang family archive.

David Godfrey-Faussett's flight logbook. *By permission, Lang family archive.*

attached to HMS *Condor* at the same time and must have been among the first to learn of his death. Having served together in *Ark Royal* for so long and seen action together in the Mediterranean, Norway and the North Atlantic, they had been extremely good friends: the loss would have been a devastating blow to my father. He rarely spoke of his friend, and I can understand why.

It is therefore an enormous privilege to be invited to write the foreword to this book about my godfather's father. Moreover, given the circumstances of the link between us, how could I possibly refuse?

Biographies about those who have served in the military tend to concentrate on a successful and influential career or involvement in a specific operation or campaign. Detailed accounts that focus on an individual's early days or time spent in a subordinate position are less common and, at face value, less interesting. From time to time however, personal records in the form of journals, letters and diaries from a bygone era emerge from long-forgotten archives or a dusty trunk at the back of an attic.

John Johnson-Allen's book draws heavily on such a find. Even a casual glance at this collection of letters is a joy. It is an extraordinary record of a cadet and midshipman in the Victorian navy, and opens a window on life in an era when the passage of time is marked by the receipt and dispatch of periodic letters to and from home.

Junior naval officers were encouraged, and indeed required, to develop their power of observation and expression as well as the habit of orderliness while serving afloat. This book brings together the fulfilment of these aims. The letters record, on a near-daily basis, the events of a voyage from Plymouth to West Africa and then to southern Africa in HMS *Dido* at the time of the Zulu wars. She was a wooden-built sloop powered by both sail and steam to produce on a good day about 11 knots, but whose average speed was in the order of 5½ knots.

As the voyage progresses, the reader begins to know and, indeed like, the young Godfrey-Faussett. Although still a teenager, he writes well, with an eye for a good story. His more engaging letters cover the port calls made and the people he meets both ashore and afloat. His sense of humour shines through much of his writing, and he was very evidently a congenial colleague among his shipmates, and highly regarded by those senior to him. Common themes include his interest in animals, both dead and alive, and we are introduced to monkeys, a leopard, a turtle and wild buffaloes, and even the cockyollie bird.

This book will, I know, give many people great pleasure. Some of it is very funny, but above all it gives an absorbing insight into how people lived and thought around 150 years ago. With his engaging manner, sense of fun and interest in everything he encounters, it isn't very difficult to understand why Midshipman Godfrey-Faussett became, later in his career, such a successful equerry to three monarchs in succession.

Rear Admiral John Lang DL

Introduction

I first came across Bryan Godfrey-Faussett when I was researching for my last book (see Bibliography). He was, in 1901, the aide-de-camp to Prince George for a royal tour in HMS *Ophir*, and kept a detailed journal of the tour. He was a compulsive diarist, and wrote journals and diaries throughout his life; his archive, held at Churchill College, Cambridge, runs to 43 boxes of files.

The early files contain his diaries and journals of his life in the Royal Navy. Amongst his diaries and his midshipman's logs were two volumes containing his transcriptions of the letters he had written to his parents and other members of his family.

His midshipman's log, which all midshipmen were required to keep, is a record of the ship's movements on a daily basis, and is a record of positions, weather and other matters relating to the management of the ship. His diaries, which he started to keep when given a diary at Christmas 1879, then sent out by post, and parts of which he includes in one of his letters, are brief details of his daily life.

He had joined HMS *Dido* in June 1879. He was 15 years old – his 16th birthday was at the end of October. His letters are the letters of a young man on his first ship, in an entirely masculine world, and they describe very clearly his life as a midshipman, both at sea and ashore. His experiences, including deaths on board, hunting wild animals in the bush in West Africa, and being entertained by the Governor of South Africa and his family, are wide and varied.

In the late 19th century, letters from and to home were the only means of communication for individuals.[1] They still were, when I went to sea at a similar age in the 1960s as an apprentice in the Merchant Navy. I visited some of the same ports that he describes, although I did not have the wide range of experiences. The weather, however, was the same as what he endured, and it was still very uncomfortable.

John Johnson-Allen

---

1 Although the electric telegraph had been in operation since around 1840, this was restricted to official communications only.

1: The Life of Bryan

Captain Sir Bryan Godfrey Godfrey-Faussett, GCVO CMG

Bryan was born on 30 October 1863 in Waterford in Ireland, of an Irish mother and an English father. His mother's family lived at Rockenham in Co. Cork, and Bryan spent his early years in Waterford. His father's family hailed from Kent, and although they had been major landowners, the divorce of his grandmother had led to the sale of the family estate, Heppington, in 1874; it had contained a large collection of old masters and other fine paintings.

This event, which took place 11 years after Bryan was born, resulted in the future for him and his siblings becoming less secure, so he was sent to Stubbington School, near Portsmouth. This was a crammer dedicated to preparing boys for the entrance examination to enter the Royal Navy and become cadets in HMS *Britannia*, the training ship moored in the River Dart, which was the forerunner of Britannia Royal Naval College at Dartmouth. Bryan passed the entrance examination successfully, although without distinction. Examinations at that time were not as searching or rigorous as they later became.

The navy that he entered had changed little since the Battle of Trafalgar. The appearance of the ships was a matter of the greatest importance and of considerable rivalry. Promotion depended more on the appearance of the ship both externally and internally than on its ability to fight a battle. This meant that wealthy officers who could afford such extravagances as gold leaf, brass finials for the ships and boats and enamel paint had an advantage over less well-off officers. The result of this spit-and-polish was that 'there is no doubt that on Sunday morning the whole ship presented a blaze of splendour to the captain as he went on his round of inspection'.[2]

This, then was what awaited Bryan when in 1877 he joined HMS *Britannia* at Dartmouth. It had been a three-deck ship of the line which had been turned into a training ship for officers in 1858, and had been joined in 1864 by the two-deck HMS *Hindustan*, moored close to *Britannia*, to provide extra accommodation. The education was similar to that taught in public schools, although there had been unfavourable press comments about the standards of education. Only five years after Bryan arrived, an article in *The Times* had claimed 'that subjects taught were inappropriate, age entry was too low and the entrance examination all wrong'.[3] The response from the Admiralty was a 'hands

---

2 Peter Padfield, Rule Britannia: the Victorian and Edwardian Navy (London 2002) p. 197.

3 Capt John Wells: *The Royal Navy*, 40

off' attitude, to the extent of regarding criticism as impertinence. Further criticism on the standards at *Britannia* came from a Captain Bowden Smith, who was in command there in the same year, who firmly believed that the 13-year-old entry excluded boys who developed later or who had not decided on the Navy as a career at 12 years old, because, as he stated, 'we want the best men we can get to officer the Navy, and by cutting off the supply at such an early age we may be losing valuable services'.[4] The theoretical subjects that the young Mr Godfrey-Faussett (as we must now call him) was taught were mathematics (arithmetic, algebra and geometry), physics, plain and spherical trigonometry, practical and theoretical navigation, charts, instruments, French, essay and drawing. In addition, and most importantly, seamanship, which attracted as many marks in the final examination as the three branches of mathematics. Although drawing

Bryan Godfrey-Faussett
at Royal Naval College Dartmouth

may not seem an obvious subject, it was naval officers who provided the Hydrographic Department with sketches of coast and port entrances for inclusion in Admiralty Pilots and on charts. In the years before photography was available to most, these were an important addition to safe navigation.

Amongst those joining shortly afterwards were the two sons of the Prince of Wales, Prince George and Prince Albert, and Rosslyn Wemyss, all of whom he would form lifelong friendships with. However, it was his friendship with Prince George which would mould his future life.

After completing his training at *Britannia*, he was appointed to HMS *Dido* in mid-June 1879, and his first letter is dated the 16th of that month, a day before they sailed for the West Coast of Africa. He remained on board *Dido* until June 1881, when he transferred to HMS *Northumberland,* an elderly ship built in 1866, one of a class of three large armoured frigates. One of the (few) high points in her career was as one

---

4 Capt John Wells: *Ibid.* 40

of two ships which towed a floating dry dock to Bermuda. She had originally been fitted with five masts, but despite this could only make a top speed of 7 knots under sail; unsurprisingly, then, she and her sister ships were described by one Admiral as 'the dullest performers under canvas of the whole masted fleet of this day and no ships ever carried so much dress to so little purpose'.[5] From HMS *Northumberland*, his next ship was HMS *Sultan*, in which he completed his training as a midshipman and was promoted to acting sub-lieutenant. His next appointment was to the Royal Naval College at Greenwich for a year's study. The proximity of Greenwich to the bright lights of London were, as they were to many young officers, a great draw. From there he moved to the Royal Naval College at Portsmouth to take the technical courses which had to be passed before promotion to lieutenant was possible. The high spirits of young officers on these courses was evidenced by a report which noted:

> an incident took place about which the Admiralty papers have now been destroyed. From the entry in the register is, it appears that Mr F.J. Proctor, editor of 'Chat' (a Portsmouth paper founded in October 1884) was assaulted by certain Sub-Lieutenants studying at Royal Naval College Portsmouth. Mr Anthony F. Gurney (the late Captain Gurney who died on 30 August 1909) was fined five pounds by the civil power; and the Commander-in-Chief, Admiral Sir Geoffrey Phipps Hornby, apparently took a dim view of the disorderly conduct of the Sub-Lieutenants. Instructions were given for all leave to be stopped, and a letter expressing Their Lordships' extreme displeasure was sent to all involved.

> Churchill College Archive WYMS1/2

After completing his studies at Portsmouth he had a brief spell in command of a sail-training brig, training cadets in the then dying art of handling sails. He was then appointed to HMS *Agamemnon* in the Mediterranean fleet as sub-lieutenant. Finally, in 1887, he was promoted to lieutenant, a pivotal step in any naval career.

In 1892, after two appointments as lieutenant, Godfrey-Faussett was asked by Prince George to join his command for a summer cruise, HMS *Melampus*.

---

5 Admiral G.A. Bullard: *The Back Battlefield*, p. 26.

ILLUSTRATED LONDON NEWS, JULY 23, 1892.—104

THE DUKE OF YORK AND H.M.S. MELAMPUS.
The ship now under the command of his Royal Highness the Duke of York, H.M.S. Melampus, belongs to the first division of the "Red Fleet," commanded by Vice-Admiral H. Fairfax, in the Naval Manœuvres appointed to take place from July 12 to July 28. The Melampus is a twin-screw cruiser of the second class, unarmoured saving a deck protected by two-inch

H.M.S. MELAMPUS.

steel plate; she was built at Barrow-in-Furness, by contract, and was launched two years ago. The hull is constructed of steel; its dimensions are: length, 300 ft.; breadth of beam, 43 ft.; draught, 16 ft. 6 in.; displacement of water, 3400 tons. The engines are, together, of 8000-horse power, working the two screw-propellers so as to attain a possible speed of twenty knots an hour; the ship carries 400 tons of coal, sufficient for steaming 8000 knots at the speed of ten knots an hour. The cost of this ship was £171,635. Her armament consists of two six-inch breech-loading rifled guns, six quick-firing guns of 4·7 in. calibre, and eight six-pounders, one three-pounder quick-firing, four machine-guns, two fixed torpedo-tubes, and two launching torpedo-carriages. The Melampus was recently commissioned at Portsmouth, and has been furnished with special cabin and state-room accommodation for his Royal Highness. Our Illustrations of the ship and portraits of the officers, from photographs by Messrs. Russell and Sons, have some interest at the present time. The Melampus is one of the seventeen cruisers, of the same class, ordered for construction by the present Board of Admiralty in 1889, including the Indefatigable, Latona, Pique, Spartan, Sirius, Naiad, Terpsichore, Thetis, and Tribune, built by private contractors, and several built in the royal dockyards.

H.M.S. MELAMPUS: THE PRINCE'S DINING-ROOM.

Press clipping showing HMS *Melampus* including internal view.

Melampus was Prince George's second command, as he'd previously had command of HMS *Thrush*, a small gunboat stationed in Canada.

Godfrey-Faussett joined *Melampus* on 29 June 1892 as third lieutenant, together with another friend from *Britannia*, Charles Cust (later Sir Charles), also a lieutenant. The ship was commissioned that day, and the crew also all joined. On the following day he was invited to a dinner at Admiralty House with the Commander-in-Chief Portsmouth, Commander Prince George, HRH Duke of York, and 12 other guests. He commented that he knew no one apart from Prince George and one other.

From Portsmouth *Melampus* sailed in the English Channel and Irish Sea, returning to the Solent for Cowes Week, where she hosted Queen Victoria, who sat on the quarterdeck to watch the sailing. The summer cruise ended on 2 September when the ship was paid off. Bryan left the ship and went by train to Monmouth to meet his family, who were staying nearby.

In February 1893 he was appointed as flag lieutenant to Admiral Sir Henry Stephenson, whose flagship was the new cruiser *Royal Arthur*. It is very likely that his appointment was helped by his friendship with Prince George. *Royal Arthur* sailed to Vancouver Island, on the west coast of Canada, to take up her station. The passage took three months, crossing the Atlantic, rounding Cape Horn and then sailing up the coasts of South, then North, America. She was on station there until June 1896, when she sailed for home, retracing her steps. It had been a challenging but enjoyable time, as Admiral Stevenson was a hard taskmaster.

On his return to England, in 1896, Godfrey-Faussett was appointed to HMY *Osborne*, the smaller and most elderly of the royal yachts in use at that time. She was a paddle steamer, and mainly transported the Prince and Princess of Wales and their children on short passages between Osborne House, on the Isle of Wight, and the mainland, or around the United Kingdom and to nearby continental ports. She spent considerable periods of time alongside in Portsmouth, particularly through the winter, where only one lieutenant was required to be on board, so it is possible that Godfrey-Faussett may have had a considerable amount of leave. Despite *Osborne*'s age, in the spring of 1897 she carried Princesses Victoria and Maude, the daughters of the future King Edward VII, to Copenhagen for Maude's marriage to Prince Charles of Denmark, who later became King Haakon VII of Norway. Despite a very rough passage across the North Sea, she arrived safely at Elbe to transit the Kiel Canal. There is no note of the ability of the princesses to cope with heavy weather in a small paddle steamer.

After his time in *Osborne*, his next appointment was at as first lieutenant

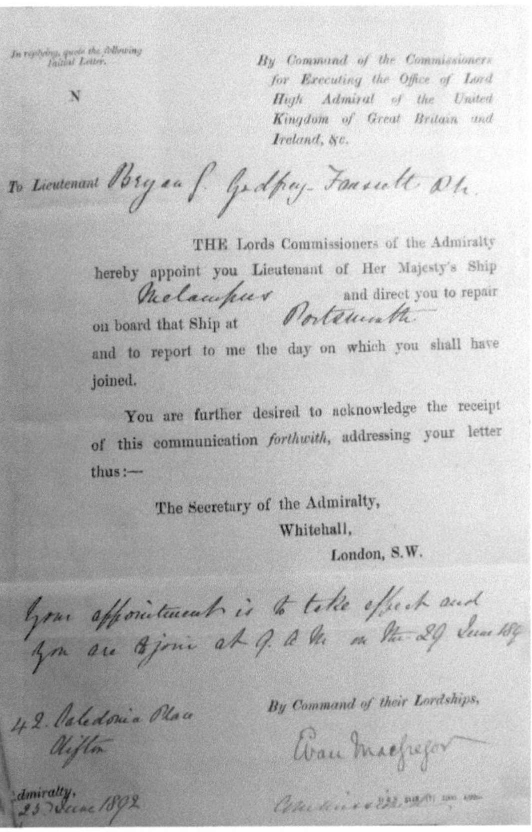

Letter of appointment to HMS *Melampus*.

Officers of HMS *Melampus*: BG-F front row, 1st left; HRH Duke of York, front row, 3rd from right

on the new battleship, HMS *Caesar*, at the end of 1897. Eighteen months later he was promoted to commander, at the age of 36. Later that year he was invited by Prince George to serve as his aide-de-camp on his future visits to the Commonwealth and Dominions. He accepted the invitation with enthusiasm. In 1901 he accompanied Prince George and Princess Mary on a royal tour to Australia and other parts of the Commonwealth and Dominions. This was to take place on board HMS *Ophir*, which had been 'taken up' by the Royal Navy for the purpose. She was one of the smaller passenger ships of the Orient Line, but still had accommodation sufficiently large and comfortable for the royal couple and their entourage. They sailed from Portsmouth on 16 March, seen off by the King and Queen on board HMY *Alberta*. The tour was an enormous success, visiting Malta, Colombo (Godfrey-Faussett noted in his journal of the tour 'on our way perspiring to Colombo'), Singapore and Australia; this was the main reason for the tour, in order for Prince George to be present at the opening of the first Commonwealth Parliament. They then travelled to New Zealand, and then back across the southern Indian Ocean to South Africa from where they crossed the Atlantic to the West Indies. On the crossing Bryan noted in his journal that he was

> rather anxious about our shirts; the capability of this ship's laundry are
> very limited indeed and if one succeeds in getting four shirts washed in
> a fortnight one is lucky.

Such were the trials of an aide-de-camp!

From the West Indies they sailed to Canada, where the royal party, including Godfrey-Faussett, left the ship and travelled the breadth of Canada, from the East Coast to the West by train over a three-week period. They sailed from St John's in Newfoundland on 11 October to return to England. Whilst on that passage Prince George invited Godfrey-Faussett to become an equerry. This, meaning that he would be seconded from the Royal Navy for an initial period of three years, effectively ended his naval career. *Ophir*'s second-in-command, Godfrey-Faussett's friend from *Britannia*, Rosslyn Wemyss, was invited to become an extra equerry, an honorary post. He too was a close friend of Prince George, and remained so for the rest of his life. On arrival in Portsmouth, the ship was greeted by the King and Queen. A dinner in the royal yacht *Victoria and Albert*, with the royal family, was held. Later in the evening on board *Ophir*, Rosslyn Wemyss was told that in recognition of the success of the tour he was to be promoted to captain and made MVO.

Godfrey-Faussett was initially appointed as an equerry-in-ordinary. One of his early roles was in 1904, when he accompanied Prince George and Princess Mary (who, following the death of Queen Victoria three years previously, had become the Prince and Princess of Wales) to the opening of the Royal Naval College at Osborne House on the Isle of Wight. Before her death Queen Victoria had granted permission for Osborne

House to be the site for the new college. The official opening took place on 18 March 1904. This was an opportunity for him to meet his old friend, Rosslyn Wemyss, who he had last seen on the *Ophir*. In the photograph Godfrey-Faussett is at the right-hand end of the back row.

Royal visit to Osborne. BG-F is at the right hand end of the back row.

His first tour abroad was to accompany Prince George and Princess Mary on their visit to India in 1905–1906. One of the highlights of this tour was an event in which he took part, rounding up a herd of wild elephants.

In 1906 he was promoted to captain and then placed on the Retired List of officers, on 31 October. Before the end of that year he had met his future wife, Eugenie Dudley-Ward. They were married on 11 April 1907, and had two sons. Whereas the elder, George, served in the Grenadier Guards with distinction in the Second World War, his younger brother, David, followed his father's footsteps and joined the Royal Navy, becoming a pilot in the Fleet Air Arm. He was the pilot of one of the two Swordfish torpedo bombers which, having taken off from the aircraft carrier HMS *Ark Royal*, attacked and disabled the steering gear of the *Bismarck* in May 1941, which proved decisive in her eventual sinking. However in 1942 David was killed in a flying accident.

In 1911 Godfrey-Faussett returned with the then King and Queen for their visit to

India, for them to be crowned Emperor and Empress of India on 12 December of that year. Whilst on this tour he took part in tiger shoots in Nepal, killing one himself – his keenness for game shooting had showed itself in his early naval career in his letters home from *Dido*.

Three years later, on the outbreak of the First World War, and with the king's approval, he rejoined the Royal Navy, and was given the command of HMS *Thistle*, which had been a steam yacht and was part of the East Coast Auxiliary Patrol. This did not last, however, as the king's wartime duties required the services of an equerry, so Godfrey-Faussett returned to that duty and served in that capacity until the end of the war. His service as an equerry continued until King George's death in 1936. He was then, much to his surprise, reappointed as an equerry to Edward VIII for the short period before the latter's abdication. He then became an extra equerry to King George VI, throughout the Second World War, until, on 20 September 1945, shortly after the end of the war, Godfrey-Faussett died at the age of 82. He had been an equerry to three monarchs over a period of 44 years.

2: *HMS Dido*

Dido was a wooden ship with a ram bow, of a class known as Corvette. She was one of seven, the class being the smallest to be classified as such; 212 feet long, with a beam of 36 feet, she had a displacement of 1,706 tons.[6] Vessels of the Corvette class were described as being very manoeuvrable under steam, and good sea boats in bad weather conditions, yet they were faster under sail than under engine power. *Dido*, like all the others of her class, was built mainly of teak because of the shortage of oak since the Napoleonic wars, and was ship-rigged.[7] The illustration shows her masts and the horizontal yards from which the sails hung

HMS *Dido* in Plymouth Sound, June 1879.

She had a main armament of 12 guns, plus some smaller swivel guns.

---

6 That is, the space that she occupied displaced 1,706 tons of water.

7 She had three masts, all of which were square-rigged.

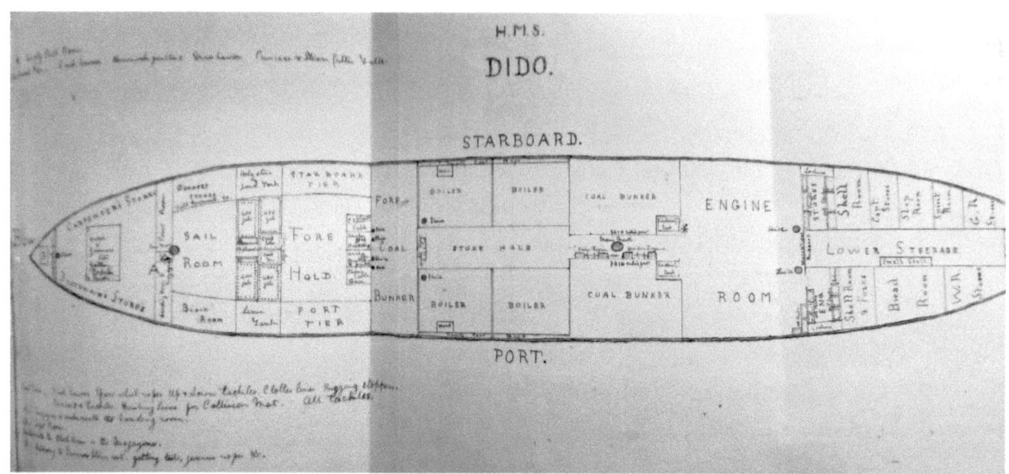

Plan of *Dido* by BG-F.

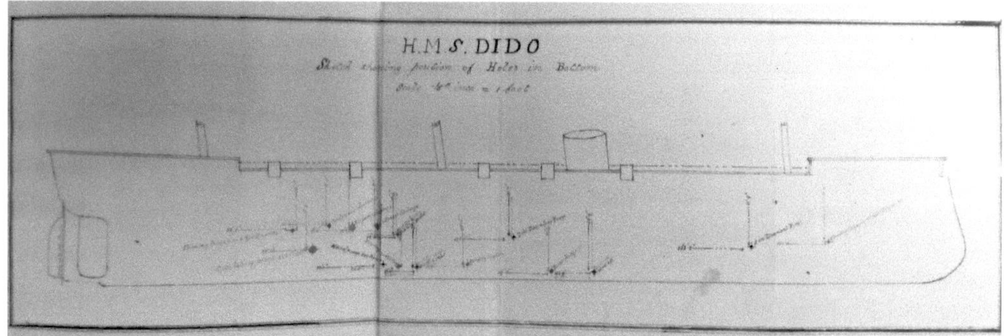

Side plan of *Dido* by BG-F.

Launched in 1869, she entered service on the West Coast of Africa, where she stayed for three years, visiting the ports and rivers that she revisited in the period that Godfrey-Faussett was on board. From the West Coast she was deployed to Australia for three years and returned to England at the end of that period. She was then decommissioned until 27 May 1879, when Godfrey-Faussett joined her. She remained in service until 1886, when she was decommissioned and all her equipment was removed so she could be used as a hulk for storage. She was eventually broken up in 1922.

The officers of HMS *Dido*. BGGF on front row, left hand end.

When Godfrey-Faussett joined her she was commanded by Captain A.R. Wright. As Godfrey-Faussett describes in his letters, Wright died on board on 19 August, some ten weeks after leaving Portsmouth. After a month under an acting captain, St Clair, a new permanent captain, Compton Domvile, was appointed. His last posting had been as captain of the Royal Naval College at Greenwich. From *Dido* he progressed in the Navy, being promoted to rear admiral in 1891, after a period as an aide-de-camp to Queen Victoria. In 1894 he was appointed second in command of the Mediterranean Fleet. Promotion to vice admiral followed in 1980. In 1897 he returned to the Mediterranean Feet as commander in chief, after promotion to admiral, replacing Admiral Sir John (Jackie) Fisher. At that time the Mediterranean feet was the largest and most prestigious in the Navy.

HMS *Dido* looking aft towards the bridge.

Compton Domvile had five children, including two sons. The elder of the two, Barry, followed his father into the Navy and also rose to the act of admiral. However, in the 1930s he became a leading British fascist and was imprisoned in 1939 as a result of his extreme views.

The Navy List of 1880 shows the officers of the *Dido*, and the midshipmen. Godfrey-Faussett refers to Thomas Atkinson alternately as chaplain or as naval instructor, which seems confusing at first, but it is clarified in the Navy List, where he is shown as both chaplain and naval instructor.

3: *Dido's commission*

Dido was commissioned into service for deployment principally to the West Coast of Africa, although with events in Southern Africa while Godfrey-Faussett was on board, she was also deployed to Natal, on the East Coast of South Africa. She visited, in total, some 20 ports or anchorages over that period. He describes the various ports from his point of view, and gives a remarkable insight into many of them.

For the navigator of the *Dido* a different source of information was available in the Admiralty *Africa Pilot*, published in three volumes. New additions were published regularly; the latest edition, published in 1875, would have been supplied to the *Dido* together with all the Admiralty charts for the areas in which she would have been operating.

The Admiralty charts of the 19th century were a comprehensive collection of charts which had all been surveyed by officers of Royal Navy vessels operating in all parts of the world during the Pax Britannica. The Admiralty Pilots, complementing the charts, gave comprehensive descriptions of the coasts, ports, navigational hazards, weather and any other factors that would help in the safe navigation of the ship. They were compiled from reports sent to the Admiralty by the fleet's navigating officers and included drawings of land features. The latest edition available to *Dido* in 1879 had been published four years before. The descriptions of the ports that follow are taken from those volumes.

These extracts from the Pilot books appear in the order in which *Dido* first visits them.

St Helena

The island appears to have suffered at different periods from the effect of volcanoes and earthquakes; and by some it has been supposed to be the shattered remains of an ancient continent connected in former ages with other rocks of the South Atlantic. The district of flat country comprising the plains of Longwood and Deadwood to the east of the island would seem to support this theory, particularly as an indigenous tree which grows here is also found on Tristan da Cunha. The remains of a vast crater are to be traced between Flagstaff Hill and the Balm on the east side of the island.

The botany of St Helena is interesting, affording nearly 60 species of indigenous trees and plants, including the tallow tree and ferns of great beauty. Trees and shrubs from all parts of the world have been collected in the gardens of Plantation House where the oak, bamboos, aloe, pine, &c. flourish together. The main ridge of the island is covered with a luxuriant vegetation of tree ferns and cabbage wood, nourished by constant moisture; and on descending from this elevation the hillsides are clothed with the richest grass, and the watercourses overhung with bramble and fuchsia; while lower down are woods of Scotch fir, larch, oak and willow.

Produce:- Provisions at St Helena are generally very dear. The lands of the island are chiefly devoted to pasturage and the gardens to the cultivation of vegetables. Coffee has been cultivated with some success and attempts made to introduce the tea plant. Sugarcane, cotton and indigo have also been tried but the rearing of cattle has been proved to be the most useful and remunerative.

Although the island is capable of supporting a large number of cattle and it has been found that the horned cattle and sheep do not in any respect degenerate from the change of climate, the demand necessitates frequent importation from the Cape of Good Hope. In the valleys by the shore, figs, oranges, pines, bananas, apples, peaches, guavas and grapes are found; and potatoes, yams, pumpkins, cabbages, peas and beans are generally plentiful. Grain crops are very uncertain, sometimes suffering from drought and always from the depredations of rats which are numerous and destructive.

Climate:- Of the climate under which such products are found, but little need be said beyond the fact of it being considered salubrious … The summer heat is not higher than in England, the temperature being kept within reasonable limits by the cold waters of the South Atlantic current; and by the trade winds which act as a constant ventilator and bring with them of a canopy of clouds sufficient to afford shelter from the vertical rays of the sun, and to admit of labour and exercise being carried on with impunity, during the heat of the day.

Population:- The population of St Helena, according to the census of 1861, amounted to 3744 males and 3086 females, making a total of 6860 ... The island possesses 16 schools having 1109 scholars.

James Bay, the port of the island, is a small indentation on the leeward side, abreast of James Valley and bounded by two high rocky hills. The space enclosed between these heights is of a triangular form ... In this confined spot is situated Jamestown which is entered from the sea side through an arched gateway within which, on the left, is the Government house and on the right the church, a plain but not inelegant building with a remarkable needle-shaped spire which forms a conspicuous object from the anchorage ... The residences of the principal inhabitants are built on the higher and cooler parts of the island, and one of the handsomest of these villas is Plantation House, an elegant mansion belonging to the Governor, situated in the midst of extensive grounds, adorned with a variety of tree and shrubs.

Longwood, the residence of Napoleon Buonaparte, stands on the plateau of Longwood, towards the east of the island, containing the greatest quantity of level ground ... The property of Longwood has lately been purchased by the Emperor of the French to whom, and his heirs, it has been conveyed in perpetuity. A French officer resides on the estate as guardian.

The only landing places are in Rupert's Bay and St James's Bay. On the shore of the former, facing the sea, stands a strong battery mounted with heavy guns ... James Valley is defended by works extending across the head of the bay, flanked by a high inaccessible battery close under which all vessels wishing to anchor in James Bay must pass.

Ascension Island

This island of volcanic origin is situated in the south Atlantic Ocean. It is of an elliptical form, its greater diameter, from east to west, being 7½ miles and shorter from north to south, little more than 6 miles. The island was first discovered on May 20 (Ascension Day) 1501 by João de Nova Gallego, a Portuguese, and was visited two years afterwards by

Alfonzo de Albuquerque, who gave it its present name.

The surface of the island is exceedingly irregular and from the sea presents a rugged and uninviting appearance. The greatest elevation is the peak of Green Mountain, so-called from the colour of its summit, which is 2820 feet above the sea and may therefore be seen from a frigate's deck at a distance of 65 miles. The principal cultivation is on the Green Mountain, where the rains fall more frequently than on the less elevated parts of the island. The principal garden is 2500 feet above the sea and here the climate is delightful, the average temperature during the day being about 75° [24°C], whilst at the landing place it is usually 85° [29°C].

In the year 1815 the British government deemed it requisite to take possession of the island of Ascension; and in 1821 the garrison was formed of a company of Marines, and by detachments from this corps the improvements on the island have been conducted. In 1823 a fever of the most virulent kind was introduced to the island by HMS *Bann*, which for a while put a stop to the improvements; the population at this time amounted to 150, of which number one third died in a very short time, whilst the crew of the *Bann*, encamped on the plain, suffered in still greater proportion. In a few months the fever, which was of the same character as the yellow fever of the West Indies, seems to have expended its power, the tone and health of the island was restored and Ascension has not since suffered from a similar visitation.

Fruits such as pines, Indian gooseberries and plantains have been successfully cultivated, and potatoes, onions, carrots, peas, French beans and almost every succulent vegetable have also been produced.

Only two deaths from sickness occurred at Ascension during the previous two years; and the value of the island as a rendezvous depot for stores and provisions began to be recognised; stock, seeds et cetera were imported from England, and horses from one of the Cape Verde Islands.

Since 1833 improvements have been steadily on the increase and so great has been the supply of water from the Green Mountain to the covered tanks as to permit the establishment to be increased to 500 or

600 souls, if required, but at present there are only 180 people living on island, the whole of whom are under the control of the Governor, who is a Captain in the Royal Navy and borne on the books of the guard ship at the cape of Good Hope. The island was formerly the headquarters of the West Coast of Africa Squadron, and depots of stores, provisions and coal were formed for the use of the cruisers and a small steam factory erected, but as the slave trade has been destroyed, the number of vessels employed in its suppression having greatly reduced, the headquarters has been removed to the Cape of Good Hope.

Turtles:- Ascension is visited by the sea turtle between Christmas and summer, and it is supposed that during the above each female makes three or four nests. The animal remains on the coast until 50 or 60 eggs are fit to be deposited in the sand and then lands on the beach between ten at night and four in the morning. She then proceeds 150 or 200 yards above high water mark, digs a large pit about eight or ten feet in diameter and two or three feet deep, in which the eggs are deposited and carefully covered over with sand; the process of incubation being left to nature. In nine or ten weeks the young turtle breaks his prison and working its way through the sand gains the surface and immediately takes to the sea after which they are never seen again until they are full grown.

Charles Darwin noted 'how can we account, for instance, for the turtles which formerly congregated in multitudes, only at one season of the year on the shores of the island of Ascension, finding their way to that speck of land in the midst of the great Atlantic Ocean?' (Quoted in *Navigation News*, November/December 2023).

Animals:- The animals indigenous to the island are wild cats and goats; rats and land crabs also abound. The cats are numerous, but instead of destroying the rats, they prey on the sea-fowl that frequent the island to lay their eggs. The goats, rats and land crabs, being enemies to cultivation, are destroyed whenever the opportunity offers, and will probably be ultimately extirpated. The insect tribe are dreadfully annoying; flies are so numerous that at mealtimes they blacken the tablecloth; ants and mosquitoes are innumerable, whilst scorpions,

centipedes, large spiders and crickets abound. The only attractive insect
is the Mountain Butterfly.

Cape Coast Castle

The castle of Cape Coast (a simple corruption of the original Portuguese
name, Cabo Corso), is built on a rock which stands on a projecting
point of the line of the shore. From the landing place the ground rises
gradually to the castle, which contains the official residences, with
the chapel, school, hospital and storehouses, beside the hall of justice.
There are also several spacious water tanks from which vessels are
occasionally supplied, but only by permission. At a short distance from
the castle three detached forts, named Fort Victoria, Fort McCarthy, and
Fort William, are situated on commanding hills.

The town, named by natives Igua, occupies a considerable space to the
northward of the castle; and besides long lines of native huts contains
some handsome European houses; the Episcopalian church and
Wesleyan Chapel are the most conspicuous public buildings. Tabara
rock is the native name for the great mass of granite on which the
castle stands, and a large solitary stone standing on the beach about ⅓
of a mile west of the castle is known as Tabara's Wife. A little further
westward there is a small saltwater lagoon which is only separated
from the sea by the ridge of the beach; at the south-west corner of the
lagoon there is a little sandy hillock named Mount Edgecumbe [*sic*].
The number of inhabitants of Cape Coast Castle is about 10,000,
almost all of whom are natives. There is a public hospital maintained by
Government; also a permanent hospital for the treatment of contagious
diseases.

Accra

Accra Point is formed by a large rock, with its southern extremity (on
which Jamestown fort is built), rising only 36 feet above high water.
The fort is nearly square in shape, about 145 feet each way with regular
bastions, and has a tall flagstaff.

The town, extending north-east and north-west from the fort, consists of several narrow streets of native dwellings and some good houses belonging to the English merchants. Westward of the town there are some brackish pools of water, which stagnate after the rainy season.

There is a constant communication between Accra and the Ashantis, who bring from the interior the greater part of the gold which is exported from this place; the country, so far as the high range of hills recently mentioned, is a fine open plain with a light soil covered with shrubs and not much heavy timber. The distant hills are covered with dense forests, but the valleys between them are described as fertile and beautiful.

On the eastern side of Jamestown Fort, between 600 and 700 yards from it, are the ruins of the fort of Crèvecoeur. It stands upon a rocky cliff about 50 feet above high water, and appears to have been of an octagonal form with a large enclosed space adjoining, which was probably the slave yard. At 2 miles eastward of Jamestown fort the Castle of Christiansborg stands upon a rocky point about 35 feet above high water; its principal part approaches the form of a square of about 190 feet in the side. On each side of it the beach forms a small sandy bay, and in front there are a few ledges of rock on which the sea breaks heavily.

There is a good road between the castle and Accra, with trees on each side which render it an agreeable walk or drive, and midway is Victoriaborg where are the public offices, post office, et cetera.

The native town, which lies northward of the castle, has not a very clean appearance; to the westward of it there is a Martello tower on a small sandy eminence and also a black wooden windmill. Farther inland there are a few detached dwelling houses.

Cattle fruit, fruit, vegetables, water and other supplies may be obtained at Accra. Fish may be caught in abundance at the anchorage. There is a contract for provisions here.

Freetown

The capital of Sierra Leone and the seat of Government was founded in 1792 and is built on rising ground sloping from the hill on which stands Government House, which, being surrounded by trees, is not easily recognised from seaward; south of this hill, on an elevated plateau, 400 feet above high water, are situated the hospital and barracks. The streets are wide but unpaved, the houses mostly constructed in European style, and it is the residence of the principal civil and military authorities. The population in 1875 was over 30,000.

Coal and Supplies:- From 5000 to 7000 tons of coal is generally in-store, and about 300 tons can be taken on board in a day or 400 working day and night. Provisions and water can be obtained from the depot at Freetown; a small pipe is led to the landing stage, but it is cheaper to hire a lighter to procure water.

Brass River

Also known as the Rio Bento or St. John, is located 9 miles east of Palm Point and 4 miles east of Cape Foremoso [*sic*], midway between the Nun entrance and west point of Brass River there are two trees, close together, which may be seen over the bush. The Brass River is formed by several branches of the main Niger, one of which, Ekole creek, is navigable for steam launches of 4½ feet draught.

In 1838 the boats of HMS Viper ascended brass River for about 60 miles and found it 400 yards wide and 9 or 10 fathoms deep, its banks fringed with impenetrable mangroves. On returning they kept along the western shore with a favourable current running 7 knots an hour [*sic*].

Settlement:- The consulate is situated on the east bank of the river, a little more than a mile inside East Point, and factories extend for more than half a mile on either side of it; this is the headquarters of the Niger Coast Protectorate. The mission house, situated 200 yards from the beach, is the most southern building, being ¼ mile from East point; and the telegraph station, the most northern, is one and three-quarter miles from the same point.

Supplies:- Bullocks, a few fowls and eggs may be procured at Tua town. Fresh water depends on the supply the resident traders have for themselves. Rainwater is used for drinking, the well water not being recommended. A doctor generally resides at the factories.

Jella Koffi or Jellu-kofi

Situated north-eastward of Cape St Paul, or midway between that Cape and Kitta, when made from the eastward, appears as several islands, the western of them being the clump of trees among which the huts and houses are built. The position of Jella Koffi is known by two large posts, painted white, which stand at the foot of a cutting into the wood and mark the entrance into the village.

Supplies:- Cattle and poultry are abundant in the vicinity of Cape St Paul and may be procured without difficulty from the natives at Weh, Jella Koffi and Kitta.

Landing:- The surf is much too high along the beach to employ ordinary boats for this purpose, but at Kitta landing is easy at times.

The Naval Contractor lives at Jella Koffi, the station near which he resides, being situated about 2 miles south of Kitta Fort; it consists of two white houses and a flagstaff.

Kitta

From Jella Koffi the shore trends about NNE for 3¾ miles to Kitta, where there is a fort having a dwelling house built on it; coming from the southward nothing can be seen of the fort, and when abreast of it only the dwelling house, which is white, and a flagstaff are visible, the fort itself being hidden by trees; just north of it there is a magazine, which is a yellow building with a white-roofed sentry box near it.

Four large houses on the beach, the southern with a very white roof, and a conical roof to its porch, serve to identify this place; the northernmost house, which is a hospital, has also a white conical roof when seen from the eastward.

From Kitta to a mile westward of the white house, which stands at
the foot of a wooded eminence with very gradual slopes, the beach is
almost clear of trees. A number of huts lie on the southern side of the
fort, and there are several narrow streets with little picketed enclosures,
some of which appear to be neatly kept; the edge of the lagoon is with
within 350 yards of the fort to the north-westward.

Supplies:- The natives at Kitta are extremely civil, and will procure
supplies if required.

Hospital:- The government maintain a public hospital at Kitta.

CAUTION:- It must be borne in mind while at anchor at Kitta, or
on this part of the coast, that tornadoes often blow onshore. Vessels
intending to stay should not anchor in less than 6 fathoms of water, as
rollers may come in unexpectedly and sometimes heavily.

Bight of Biafra

General remarks:- The islands in the Bight of Biafra are four in
number, and nearly equidistant; the north-eastern, inner, and largest
island is Fernando Po; the two central being Princes and St Thomas
islands, whilst the outer and south-western isle is known as Anno Bom.
All these islands, as well as the lofty ranges on the mainland within
Fernando Po, are evidently of volcanic origin, and are probably the
gigantic results of submarine upheaval.

Fernando Po

This island, which from its size and geographical position is the most
important in the Bight of Biafra, … is rectangular in form, with a length
of 35 miles NE and SW, and a mean breadth of 17 miles. The island was
discovered in 1471 by a noble Portuguese named Fernado-Poo, after
whom it was called; its present appellation therefore is a corruption of
the proper name. The island is now a Spanish possession, having been
exchanged by treaty in 1778 for the island of Trinidad off the eastern
coast of Brazil.

A ridge of mountains traverses nearly the whole length of the island, and culminates in a magnificent cone, called Clarence Peak, the summit of which is 10,190 feet above the sea, and almost constantly enveloped in clouds. It has been considered doubtful whether the peak can yet be considered extinct, as smoke is said to have been occasionally seen, but the highest parts, composed of volcanic scoria, have been so decomposed as to be covered with a grassy vegetation.

When seen from seaward, the island of Fernando Po is one of the most beautiful objects in the world. Clarence Peak is visible on a clear day or after a tornado from a distance of 100 miles from the westward, but generally the weather is so hazy as to prevent its being seen beyond 3 or 4 miles. There are also two smaller peaks near the south-west extremity of the island, but of diminutive height when compared with their stupendous neighbour. The channel separating Fernando Po from the base of the Cameroon Mountains on the mainland is 19 miles across, and from mid-channel the appearance of the magnificent mountain masses on either side is most grand and impressive

In 1827 the Spanish government permitted the English to form an establishment for the purposes of supplying provisions and stores to the British squadron employed in suppressing the slave trade; and a settlement was accordingly formed in Clarence Cove on the north side of the island; but about 1843–4, in consequence of the unhealthy nature of the climate and expressed wishes of the Spanish government, the establishment was abandoned, and the whole island reverted to the possession of possession of Spain.

Population:- The natives of Fernando Po belong to the Adeeyah tribe but are known to the Europeans as the Boobees from their word of salutation, signifying 'stranger'; and their number at different periods has been estimated from 7,000 to 10,000. They are a peculiar race and differ in their physical characteristics and language from their continental neighbours, though they retain, in a modified degree, the superstitious prejudice and debasing customs which characterise the natives of the mainland.

Although of an unprepossessing appearance, and warlike among themselves, they are said to be friendly, hospitable and forbearing to white men, whilst in physical confirmation they are as a rule well made and muscular.

Products and Supplies:- The forests of Fernando Po produce a great variety of trees, of which many are very valuable for shipbuilding and commercial purposes. Amongst others beside the palm, are the ebony, African oak, lignum vitae, yellow logwood, and many species of mahogany. … Many of these trees attain gigantic heights, and measure 150 feet from the base to the first branch, and during the dry seasons are ornamented by festoons of beautiful climbing plants pendant from the branches.

The island is much resorted to by English cruisers and palm oil vessels, to obtain supplies of wood, water and coals for steamers. Stock, however, excepting yams, is neither abundant or cheap. Green pigeons are said to be plentiful and may be shot by going a short distance into the bush and waiting for their settling on the branches of the high trees.

Batonga Bay

Would be more correctly described as an open roadstead abreast an English factory about 7 miles to the southward of Point Garajam. Landing is very dangerous, and many lives are lost in making the attempt; at times a heavy surf breaks upon the whole line of coast between Cameroon River and Corisco Bay.

The country known by the names of Batonga or Banoko – properly the names of important tribes – begins at the south shore of the innermost recess of the Bight of Biafra, and extends southward as far as Cape St John, the limit in this direction of the British consulate of Biafra.

Batonga is celebrated for its canoes, which consist of cottonwood or some other light timber, carefully hollowed out by a native adze; they are about the length of a man, rarely exceed 15 lb in weight, and are sometimes curved and decorated with red paint, and yet sell for a dollar each. The thinnest of crossbars connect the sides, and the owner sits on a curved shaped ridge of wood – a few inches above the gunwale – as on a saddle, with one leg on each side and his feet in the water: nothing can exceed the skill with which these people launch through a heavy surf, which would prove fatal to ordinary ships' boats.

Bonny River

From Rough Corner Point the coast trends NE ¾ E for 3½ miles to the factories and mission house of Bonny, a large native town. Bonny town stands on ground nowhere more than 4 feet above the river, the soil being composed of sand and decaying vegetation; there are mangrove swamps close to, and during the rainy season the site is more or less covered with water; several hulks lie aground on the beach.[8] A new Mission Chapel has been built, the old one is now the telegraph station. King Amachii's town is situated 15 miles above Bonny town.

The Consulate, a two-storey building, slate-coloured, with a red roof, is situated near the telegraph station; there is a conspicuous chapel with a spire, situated about half a mile south-west of Bonny town.

Coal and supplies:- Coal, in small quantities, may be obtained from the steamers of the British and African Company, and lighters capable of holding from 3 to 5 tons may be hired from the factories; coaling will probably be at the rate of from 8 to 10 tons per hour. There is now no coal depot. Fresh provisions are as a rule plentiful; pigeons may be shot in Boler Creek in the early morning.

Gaboon River

This river, which takes its rise among the Sierra del Crystal mountains, empties its waters into the Atlantic a few miles north of the equator. Its mouth forms a bay which is the finest harbour on the west coast of Africa, and here, on the right bank, the French formed a settlement in 1843.

The Gaboon is accessible to the largest ships, and affords commodious anchorage, and good shelter for a fleet, for although the numerous and

---

8 In 1965, when I arrived there by sea, despite by then it being an oil terminal, it seemed little changed. J. J-A.

extensive shoals which obstruct the entrance render the navigation somewhat difficult, they increase the security of the anchorage on both sides of the river. …

The shores of the right side of the Gaboon rises at Guegay Creek, and is fronted by chalky beds, which dry out a cable's length at low water. At the distance of a mile south east of the creek is Breton Point and close to the shore …, are the villages of Kringer, Quaben and Louis, with an aggregate population of about 1400; of these villages Kringer is the most important.

The Gaboon was colonised by the French in 1843, and the government establishments, situated on the right bank of the river, occupy commanding positions near the shore a little to the southward of Breton Point. The Blockhouse, erected in 1843, stands on an eminence near the shore, one third of a mile to the south-eastward of Breton Point, and near it is a convenient landing place; it has now been abandoned as a stronghold, and forms part of the garden of the Roman Catholic mission, whose church dwelling houses, schools and workshops are in the immediate vicinity. The children are well cared for, and the boys are taught some useful trade and also have an excellent band, and the girls, under the direction of a community of nuns, are instructed in domestic duties of various kinds.

The present establishment consisting of a conspicuous brick building in which the commandant, garrison, and administrative officers reside, stands on a cleared eminence on the shore side of Libreville, two thirds of a mile from the blockhouse, with which it must not be confounded as a mark for entering. Abreast the governor's house is a mole which renders landing easy; the hospital and powder magazine are both afloat.

The French establishment is independent of the government of Senegal, and the river Gaboon has become the centre of administration, supported by a naval and military force.

Contiguous to the Government house is the village of Libreville, or Freetown, founded in 1849 and inhabited by liberated blacks; and about 2 miles from the blockhouse, in a slight indentation between French and Paris points, stands the village of Glass, the principal place of trade in the whole river. Within it on a beautiful hill named Baraka – derived from Barracoon – is the American mission, with numerous buildings and spacious grounds which occupy the site of what a few years since was a noted slave factory.

Productions:- Vegetation here is magnificent, and woods of all kinds adapted for building and dyeing purposes abound. The country and soil are well adapted for the cultivation of cotton and other tropical commodities not indigenous to the country; the coffee plant has already been introduced, and sugar canes grow luxuriantly on the banks of the river, but the difficulty is to impart industrious habits to people accustomed to find sufficient produce at hand to satisfy their wants without trouble.

The chief product of the Gaboon country is its ivory, which is brought from the interior in great quantities and said to be the finest on the western coast.

Cape Lopez

This point is the southern limit of the Bight of Biafra, and, as before observed, the westernmost point of South Africa. The promontory was originally named Lopo Gonzalves by the Portuguese, and though, from its salient position, it is easy of recognition, the term 'cape' seems misapplied, for the point is composed of a low sandy beach covered with mangroves. The cape is the northern extremity of a low, wooded island 21 miles in length north and south, its greatest breadth being 4 miles; it is separated from the main shore by mouth of the Mexias River, which flows into the depth of Cape Lopez Bay, and to which the French have given the name of the River Lopez.

Supplies:- Fish are plentiful in Cape Lopez Bay, and the seine may be used with advantage around, and in the vicinity of, Death Island. Wood is obtainable, and from Fetish town, fowls' eggs and fruit may occasionally be procured.

Commerce:- The articles of commerce consist of ivory, tortoiseshell, wax, dye-wood, and ebony; mats of a superior description are manufactured by the natives. In the country around, elephants, lions, tigers and buffaloes abound, whilst in the numerous streams which intersect the coast are numerous hippopotami. The natives consider monkeys sacred, and worship them as Fetish animals.

St Thomas Island

This island, which is a Portuguese possession, is much larger than Princes Island and of greater commercial importance, but is less useful as a place of call in consequence of its want of harbours. It should not be approached by vessels which do not intend anchoring, as calms, baffling winds, and strong currents prevail in its vicinity.

The island, when seen from the north-east at a distance of 60 miles, shows as three very remarkable mountains, viz: Pico de São Thome, whose summit is most frequently hidden by clouds; the Pico Cap Grande with its needle-shaped peak, the Pico de Maria Fernandez, the top of which resembles the form of a sugar-loaf.

Population:- In 1874 the population consisted of about 18,000. The people reside principally in eight villages or towns, the principal being that of São Thome, in Anna de Chaves Bay, on the north east side of the island; but here and there some habitations are seen bordering on the shore. This being a Portuguese penal settlement, there are about 400 convicts on the island, and a regiment of black troops is also stationed here.

Produce:- The island is composed of very compact and heavy basaltic rock covered by one of the most fertile soils imaginable, but its cultivation is neglected in consequence of want of labour. Its chief exports consist of coffee and cocoa; bullocks, pigs, goats and fowls are plentiful and good, and may be obtained at moderate charges. In 1874 bullocks weighing about 300 lb each were obtained for 12 shillings a head. Excellent water and plenty of wood are procurable.

St Paul de Loando

The town is not only the capital of Angola, but is the principal city of the Portuguese dominions in South Africa. It stands at the head of the bay or port of the same name, derived from Loando Island, which shelters it from the west and presents an imposing appearance from the sea. The city was erected by the Portuguese in 1578, is a bishop's see, and is divided into a lower and higher town; it is of considerable extent and contains numerous churches, with many substantial public and private buildings, but many are in ruins and the whole town is fast falling into a state of utter decay, which may be traced to the abolition of the slave trade.

The lower town skirts the shore between Fort San Miguel and the public gardens, and consists principally of mean-looking hovels composed of wattle and daub, the residences of the free portion of the black inhabitants. The other town is naturally the healthier part, and in it are the commodious residences of the governor, the bishop, and public functionaries as well as several churches, the hospital, and the cathedral, now partly in ruins. The population, though necessarily fluctuating in numbers, consists of about 1600 whites and 3400 blacks, making a total of 5000.

The city is strongly fortified, and these safeguards are in a state of good preservation. In addition to the fort of San Pedro, which was erected between the years 1703—5, there is the handsome fortress of San Francisco de Penedo, built on the Vauban system and consisting of an irregular pentagon surrounded by two batteries, the upper mounting 24, and the lower 37 guns. This fortress commands the entrance to the port, the anchorage, and the road by which provisions are conveyed from the country to Loando.

Supplies:- The principal articles of commerce are ivory, gum-copal, orchilla and beeswax; the last-named being procured in great quantities from the interior. The daily market, which should be attended at daylight, affords an abundant supply of livestock, vegetables and fruit, which are to be obtained at a reasonable rate. The lime purchased here is of a very superior quality, and is made on the island of Loando where there is also a soap factory. Fish is plentiful, and may be caught in large quantities with the seine.

Simons Bay

Is situated 11 miles from Cape point, and near the north-west corner of False Bay. From April to September, when Table bay is considered unsafe, ships usually put into Simons bay; and in every month of the year this is a place of safety. Although open to east and north-east winds, these never blow strong, so that it is a safe retreat for vessels at all seasons.

Simons bay is an accessible harbour all year round for distressed ships, and affords complete shelter; for even with heavy south-easters ships ride safely, and these are the only winds which cause inconvenience as far as the harbour is concerned.

The dockyard, though small, is a complete establishment for its size, and is capable of refitting and provisioning the ships belonging to the station as well as casual passers-by; but if unusual supplies for transports or others be required, they have to be purchased at Cape town and some delay is occasioned whilst a sufficient quantity of biscuit is being baked. There is but little convenience at present for repairs of steam machinery.

There is an electric telegraph to Cape town, thence to Paarl, Stellenbosch and Wellington. In the course of time it is probable that a railway will be constructed to Cape town or if not that, Kalk bay will be improved as a landing place for cargoes to be discharged there and conveyed to Cape town so to get over the difficulties of carriage across the sandy beaches between Simons and Kalk bays.

Supplies:- The water in Simons bay is excellent. For men-of-war, it is brought alongside in a tank vessel containing about 70 tons. There is a smaller tank vessel, for merchant ships, containing about 5 tons, but the dockyard tank is frequently lent to water merchant ships on application. Refreshments and supplies of all kind, if in excess of what Simons town can supply, are obtained from the interior and from Cape town, distant by road 22 miles. This is abundant in the bay, and the beaches are good for hauling the seine.

CAUTION:- There is a fish in Simons bay commonly called the toadfish,[9] about six inches long; back dark, with deep black stripes, belly white, with faint yellow patches; it swims near the surface, and is a constant attendant on lines employed fishing. When taken from the water it puffs out considerably. Should any portion of the fish be eaten, *death* ensues in a few minutes.

Saldanha Bay

Close to the North point of this noble bay, Ship Rock, and thence to Stomp point, on the south side of the entrance, the distance is 4⅓ miles. Within this line, the entrance channel, which is bounded by hills of granite about 80 feet high, runs in for a distance of 3 miles but then opens out immediately into an extensive basin 6 miles in length north and south, affording good anchorage on its northern and southern shores.

Saldanha bay from its natural formation is admirably adapted for commercial purposes, and for the easy ingress of ships requiring the repair of damages sustained at sea. Indeed, it may be said to be the only safe harbour on this portion of the coast, and its natural capabilities rendered it, in the opinion of the late Sir John Barrow one of the finest harbours of the world.

The great capabilities of this fine bay as a harbour were greatly appreciated by the Dutch, who made it a station for their ships of war, and a postal rendezvous for their East Indian possessions. This place also possesses historical associations, for in August 1796, a Dutch squadron consisting of three ships of the line, five frigates and sloops, and one store ship, at anchor in Saldanha Bay, surrendered to a British squadron of superior force under Vice-Admiral Sir George Keith Elphinstone, afterwards Lord Keith.

---

9 Probably the *fugu* or pufferfish.

Cape Natal

Is a high wooded tongue of land, terminating in a remarkable bluff 195 feet high, and is easily made out, the coast to the northward falling a little back and being low for several miles. At the foot of the bluff on its eastern side, a flat rock 20 feet high and about 40 feet long projects seaward, and thence rocks which uncover at low water springs extend to the north-west towards the bar.

The bar of sand which crosses the mouth of the port is constantly changing in both direction and depth and should never be attempted by a stranger. It is silted up by the swell of the ocean, and scoured out by the force of the ebb which has been found sufficient to deepen the water 12 inches in one tide.

Durban

The town of Port Natal stands about 1½ miles from Sandy point and is about 54 miles by road from Pietermaritzburg, the capital of the colony. It is well laid out, with wide streets lined with trees. The houses are principally built of wood. Here there is an Episcopalian church and Wesleyan Chapel, banks, mechanic's institute, several clubs and societies a marketplace &c. The population in 1878 may be about 8,000, the greater part whites.

The chief exports are wool, ivory, arrowroot, butter, ostrich feathers, flower, grain, gold dust and bars, hides, red ore, skins, raw sugar, cotton, pepper, coffee, rum, &c. The sugarcane flourishes, and excellent sugar has been produced, as also has the best quality of arrowroot, and rice, ginger, turmeric, chicory, coffee and tobacco; of fruits – pineapples, mangoes, bananas, sour-sops, lemons, chillies &c. thrive, as well as potatoes and all kinds of European vegetables, also corn and oats.

Supplies:- Water and provisions may be obtained and are sent off in large boats to vessels lying in the roads outside the bar, but this is an expensive and tedious proceeding. In the harbour refreshments may be obtained at moderate prices.

4: The scrapbook

Towards the end of 1879, Bryan Godfrey-Faussett started to compile a scrapbook, cutting out pictures and other items that interested him from the newspapers and periodicals that were sent to the ship. Amongst the journals he used was the *Sporting and Dramatic Review*, to which he frequently refers. He also put in various items that interested him or appealed to him, including the Christmas cards and New Year's cards that he received, and some of his own sketches and cartoons.

The illustrations appear in the order that they are in his book. It is not clear how long he maintained it, but certainly up to his departure from HMS *Dido* in 1881.

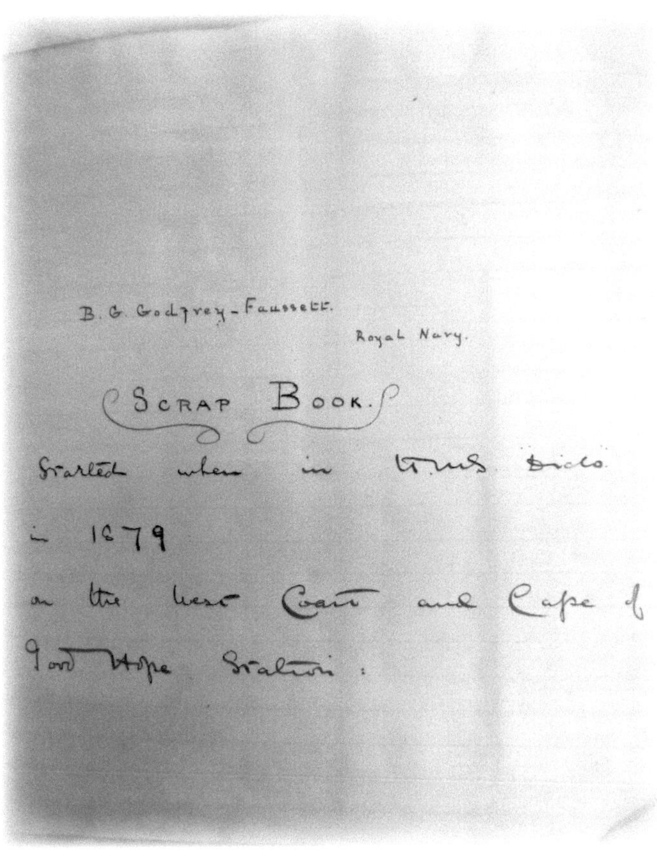

THE CHURCH PORCH, WERTHEIM

1880.
From the Sporting and Dramatic Newspaper.
FRED. ARCHER.

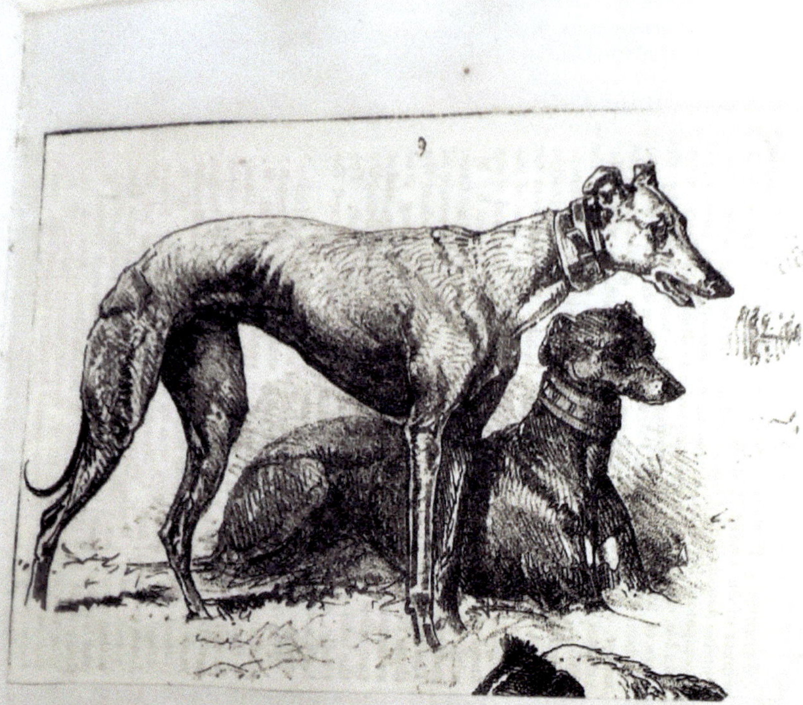

CHRISTMAS
COMPLIMENTS
of
the
SEASON

May
the New Year
bring
New Blessings

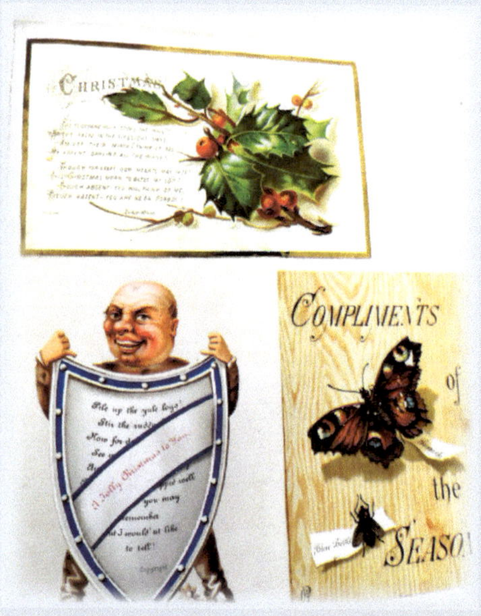

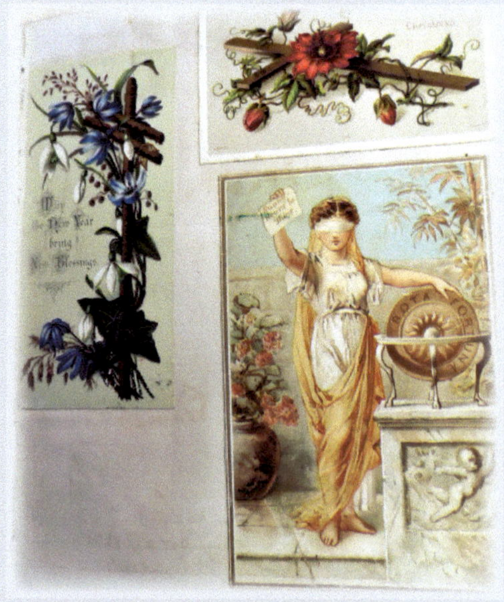

Jockey Club Cup.   Value 300£.
Run for at Houghton Meeting Oct 29ᵈ 1880

"Boadicea" at Simon's Bay.
5 May 1880.

memo

I acquaint you that I have made the following remarks relative to Her Majesty's Ship "Dido" under your command on the Report of Inspection dated 3rd. inst.

"The Ship is in all respects in a perfect state of cleanliness and order".

"The Ship's company are a fine body of young men, very clean and creditable in appearance."

"All the arrangements for battle are good and efficient."

"The general condition of discipline and order of the "Dido" reflects the highest credit on her Captain & Officers."

Signed

F. W. Richards.
C.B., A.D.C.,
Commodore.

Captain Compton E. Domvile.
H.M.S. "Dido".

The Oldest Lady Member
of the Wilderness Club

Inexperience Missed! — !! — !!!!

A BILL OF YE FAYRE.
Some Soupe yclepped Julienne.
A head of a fyne Boar.
A ryghte Kinglie Peacock, trewlie toothsome.
A graunde Turkey and Tongue withal.
Several Fowles, roasted.
Tongue from a far-off Countrie yclepped Russia.
A Pastie ; there are dyvers kyndes of Game in it.
Several Fowles, boiled—verrie goode and trewlie tender.
Ye goode olde English Sir Loin, Bart.
Some Beefe, well cooked.
Some real Yorkshire Ham.
" Alle whoe doe eate thy Ham, 'tis sayd,
Will never lack ye want of bread."
A fresh Salad ; there is a Lobster in it.
A Salad mayde as ye Russians doe make it.
Some Jellies wythe Wyne therein.
Jellies quite clare ; they taste of Oranges.
Creams mayde toothsome with Vanilla,
Some Creams that taste lyke Coffee.
Some Trifle ; thys is how ye Trifle is mixed in Switzerland.
Ye Ices—verrie collde.
Raspberrie Creame,   Vanilla Creame.
Lemon Water,

———

YE
COOLSOME AND
HARMLESS
DRYNKES.
Ye Zoedone
Verrie sparklesome.
Ye Rubine.
Ye Vin Santé.
Soda Water
and eke
Lemonade.
Maister Schweppe,
he mayde them.
Ye Ginger Ale
and ye Lemonade,
mayde by
Maisters Cantrell
&
Cochrane.
Ye Tea of Beefe.

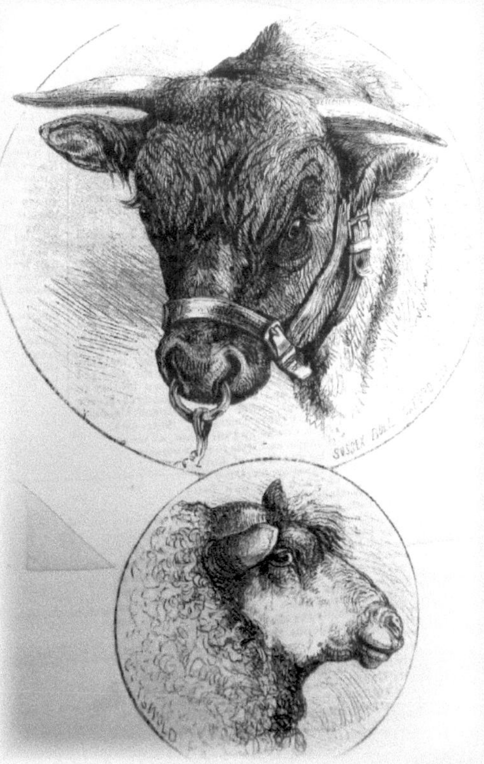

ROCKED (BUT NOT TO SLEEP.)
"A Study in Black and White" 
Viscount Sherbrooke and H.H. the Nawab Mukiwamu

MAGDALEN BRIDGE, OXFORD, THE WIDENING OF WHICH HAS BEEN

Piedigrotta, Naples.

H.M.S. "DIDO'S" MINSTRELS.
CONCERT AND NEGRO ENTERTAINMENT
IN THE
SCHOOL-ROOM, SIMON'S TOWN,
TUESDAY, 7TH JUNE, 1881.
PROGRAMME:
OVERTURE—"Inspection of Troops" ... BAND.
GLEE—"Love at Home" ... TROUPE.
SONG—"Julianna Johnson" ... MASSA STRINGS.

SELLING OFF! RETIRING FROM BUSINESS!!

Freeholds, Leaseholds, Reversionary Interests, Household Effects and Shares.

MR. W. E. GLADSTONE

Will Sell by Auction, at the BOER'S HEAD HOTEL,

On Saturday, the 1st day of April next, at noon *(Greenwich Mean Time)*,

THE WHOLE OF THE VAST

LANDED ESTATES

GOODS, CHATTELS and EFFECTS of

JOHN BULL, ESQ.,

Who is retiring from Business on account of advancing age and ill-health, induced by recent losses in his TRANSVAAL Venture, comprising

THREE KINGDOMS (United or otherwise),
ONE EMPIRE, ONE DOMINION, FORTY-EIGHT COLONIES
And ONE SUZERAINTY,

Situate as undermentioned and containing upwards of 8,982,177 Square Miles (with a total Rent Roll of £174,775,000) of good Freehold and Leasehold Land, Government Offices, Residencies, and Missionary Stations. Diamond, Gold, Silver, Coal and other mines in full operation. One large Public House known as "THE LORDS AND COMMONS."

Also an extremely Elegant, Spacious and Well-built Family Mansion, known as "BUCKINGHAM PALACE," with Greenhouses, Gardens, Stables &c., and every necessary appurtenant. The Residence contains ample Accommodation for a Family of Position, is situate in its own grounds and commands good views of the Nelson Monument, St. Paul's Cathedral and Westminster Abbey and is within easy distance of the thriving market towns of London and Westminster.

Railway Communication to all Parts close at hand.

The whole of the above extensive Properties, which are well Wooded and Watered, will be put up in one Lot, but if not thus Sold will be offered in the following Lots, viz:—

LOT 1. **Great Britain.** This Freehold Estate is comprised of the adjoining properties of **England, Wales and Scotland,** the first of which has been in the possession and occupation of the Vendor's family for a lengthened period, and on it are situated the above-mentioned Family Mansion and Public House.

NOTE:—All Trophies, notably the Russian Cannon, which have been placed in ornamental positions on this Estate, and to which the Vendor acknowledges he has no moral right will be returned to their respective owners, with apologies, if demanded at the close of the sale.

LOT 2. **Ireland.** A fine Residential Property with bullet proof Dwelling Houses and Out Buildings (this is colored green on the plan and the option of purchasing it will be first offered to the *peasant* proprietors.)

NOTE:—As the Vendor cannot disguise the fact that this is a bad lot, he will not enter into any covenant to indemnify the purchaser from loss arising from Boycotting or other sentences of the Land League Courts, but the purchaser will be entitled to appropriate any back rents he may be able to collect.

LOT 3. **India.** This magnificent Empire, purchased by the vendor at an enormous expense, would form a most desirable acquisition to neighbouring owners. The key of the Mansion may be obtained on application to Mr. ABDURRAHMAN, *Candahar Lodge,* close to the north west entrance of the demesne. There is a great variety of game on the Estate and also capital boar shooting within easy distance. In this lot is included a right of way over the Cyprus Estate.

LOT 4. **Canada.** All that well-watered Messuage, Tenement, Dominion, Hereditaments and Premises lying to the northward of the allotment ground known by the name of the " United States," formerly in the Vendor's possession.

NOTE—The present Steward of this Estate is a connection of the Vendor, and can, if necessary, remain in charge for a limited period, to suit the convenience of the purchaser.

LOT 5. Two small but conveniently situated **Island Dependencies,** known respectively as **Heligoland** and **Malta,** and a rocky Promontory called **Gibraltar.**

NOTE—All of these nice little Properties are in Europe, and would be most valuable acquisitions to an enterprising Company as Coaling Stations, or to Yacht Clubs.

LOT 6. Four semi-detached Residencies, **Aden, Hong Kong, Sarawak** and **Singapore,** and two Islands, **Ceylon** and **Labuan,** the whole known as the British Colonies in Asia.

LOT 7. All those Freehold, Leasehold and Copyhold Estates, collectively known as the **British Colonies in Africa.** This lot includes the Transvaal Farm, which is Leasehold, and the Purchaser may have at any time short notice to quit.

LOT 8. Comprises the **whole of the British Colonies in America and the West Indies.** The purchaser of this Lot will have the right of fishing over the waters of the Newfoundland Fishing Association and a Reversionary Interest in a large number of Bonds issued by the Peruvian Government.

LOT 9. Comprises the whole of the **British Colonies in Australasia.** This lot abounds in mineral wealth and also offers special attractions to sheep-farmers and others. A portion of this property is of immense interest to historians as the scene of the early labours of Arthur Orton.

LOT 10. All that choice assortment of **War Ships,** wooden, iron and plated, of the newest patterns and designs; as well as the **Great Guns, Torpedoes, &c.,** all of the Vendor's own manufacture, for which he has long been so justly celebrated, and **Marine Stores** of every description. This lot is the Finest Collection of specimens of naval architecture in the world, and includes the fine old three-decker "The Victory," which, although depreciated by the radical tendencies of the age, is still an object of respectful veneration to all admirers of the brilliant history of the present owner's family.

LOT 11. All that Choice Assortment of **Warlike Implements not included in the last Lot;** comprising Rifles (both breech and muzzle loading), Swords, Bayonets and other Accoutrements, Heliographs, Field Telegraphs, Rocket and other Apparatus, used by the British Army before its annihilation.

NOTE.—It will be observed that as the Vendor is disposing of the whole of his real estate, the property comprised in the last two Lots, hitherto used in defence of the same, will be of no further use to him.

LOT 12. **Suez Canal.** A large number of Shares in this profitable speculation recently purchased under exceptionally advantageous circumstances, and now greatly enhanced in value.

LOT 13. All those fine **Antique and Modern Robes and Jewels,** including the **Heirlooms** which have been in the family of the vendor for many centuries. Comprising—Unique Crowns, Magnificent Sceptres, Gorgeous Insignia, unrivalled Stars and Orders, matchless Gems (including the world-famed Koh-i-noor) and a quaint old **Throne** of British Oak, which, although it has braved a thousand years, is still convertible into a variety of useful family articles.

NOTE—This last lot, to which the attention of theatrical managers, actors, &c., is particularly directed, will, if necessary, be divided into small parcels to suit the convenience of purchasers.

LOT 14. A job lot of **Miscellaneous Articles,** including the Trafalgar Square Lions, the Wellington Sarcophagus, and the whole of the Historical Monuments in Westminster Abbey and St Paul's Cathedral, the old Armour and Beef-eaters in the Tower, a number of antiquated Ambassadors, as well as a large lot of minor articles too numerous to particularize.

NOTE.—It was intended to include in this Sale the Endowments and other income of the Church of England, but these will now be disposed of by private Contract.

The Auctioneer mindful of the success which attended his labours on a previous occasion, when it was his privilege to offer for Sale the Irish Ecclesiastical Property of the Vendor, confidently places himself in the hands of the public, feeling sure that a handsome competency to solace the declining years of his employer will be the result of his efforts, especially as the whole of the above will be sold without reserve.

CATALOGUES illustrated by Woodcuts, laboriously executed by the Auctioneer himself, of objects of interest in and about the Property may be had on application at office. All communications replied to immediately by post card. For Cards to View the several Properties apply to the Vendor.

THE SCOTCH TERRIER.
Scribblings by
Walter B. Barrett.
1880.

Scene in Oxford Street –
an Actress returning from Princess's.

Wyfold Cup.
Fawley Court.

OXFORD AT MAIDENHEAD - BELOW CLIEFDEN-
THE HARD WORKED

THE OURANG OUTANG AT THE WESTMINSTER AQUARIUM

5: The letters, 1879

HMS *Dido*, Plymouth Sound, Plymouth, June 16th Monday 1879

My Dear Mother

Thanks for your letter. Granny wrote to me and sent me a photo of grandpa. We are going to sail tomorrow, Tuesday, at 10 o'clock in the morning for Cape Coast Castle, calling at Madeira, perhaps, and then we are going along the coast to the Cape, calling at some places to coal et cetera. You will be able to find out by the papers and where to write et cetera. I can't help you, because we don't know for certain if we are going to call at Madeira. There is a row going on at Cape Coast Castle I believe. So that is why we have got to go there and then on to the Cape. We will be about a week, not less, before we get there.

This afternoon I had charge of a Cutter, the proper mid[10] being absent, and I had to wear my dirk. I had to take some officers onshore and then go on and take a prisoner on board the *Royal Adelaide*, with a corporal. The Commander spoke to me on the *Adelaide,* then on the way back I took a lot of provisions on board here with the steward and some others. My stations are, field gun, main top for divisions and in fire quarters midship – so if we land I shoot the Zulus. I shall have the field gun!!! We take quinine twice a day going along the Coast I believe. The ship is rolling a little but I don't feel sick yet!!! Colmore is very nice to all of us; he told me he had been asked by a lot of people to look after me, and the first lieutenant said something about looking after me. This morning we have been hard at work settling the gun room. It is very nicely fitted but very small for the number of fellows: there are 10 of us in it. Colmore and the other sub lieutenants have got guns and one of the mids, Williams, so there are four guns in the gun room; there will be some shooting at Cape Coast Castle I believe. I'm sending my portmanteau home because the first lieutenant won't allow portmanteaus to be left on board, because there is no room: it was with difficulty I could keep my bag, and my chest is crammed full so there is no room in that. I have sent some books which I was told were useless, and my Ulster,[11] which Colmore and some other chaps told me were of no use to me, and Colmore told me that he had just sent his home and if I do want it I can get it easily sent out. The ship is really rocking and I can

---

10 midshipman

11 caped overcoat *à la* Sherlock Holmes

feel it quite easily and the lamps are rocking but as I said before I don't feel sick!!! The *Dido* is painted white and it has ram bows which I am very glad of. We will go about 7 kn I think, sail if there is a fair wind or steam or both. She is a very nice looking craft indeed I think. I do not care about —, but I like all the rest of the fellows. Captain Wright is awfully jolly. I believe we are going to work in his cabin because there is no room in the gun room. The first lieutenant is also very jolly I believe. I had to pay 16 shillings for my mess on *Adelaide* and six shillings for washing altogether. We are anchored close to the *Agincourt* in the sound – you remember. Tell me if the photographer has sent you the photos – Groom, photographer, Fern St [?], would reach him I should think. I did not pay him you know. I have not got anything more from Fraser and D.... Now I must say goodbye. Good hugs to all and everyone, love to papa, yourself and the others

From your loving son

B G Godfrey-Faussett

HMS *Dido*. Just out of Bay of Biscay and off Vigo, out of sight of land, June 22, 1879, Sunday

Dear mother and papa

What on earth is going on in the world? I am sure I don't know. Is the Zulu war over, or is there another war with anybody else or what? This is like living in a cell only worse. We will get to Madeira in about four days and we started from England five days ago making nine days at sea without seeing land – well I am blessed! I will just give a list of the watches which we, the midshipmen, have to keep or are supposed to be on deck (the ship is rolling like a porpoise, so I'm writing under difficulties sitting on the chest with my blotting book on my lap). List of watches: 8:30 am to 12:30 pm, 12:30 pm to 4 pm, 4 pm to 6 pm, 6 pm to 8 pm, 8 pm to 12 pm, 12 pm to 4 am, 4 am to 8:30 am, 8:30 am to 12:30 pm. I have kept all these watches. No doubt you will be horrified. I dislike the forenoon, 8:30 am to 12:30 pm, the most because it is in the day and I cannot sit down and besides there is more to do. It is not at all nice turning out at 12 o'clock in the night going on deck for four hours to 4 o'clock and very likely a wet night. But if you have a nice officer of the watch he lets you go below into the gun room then you only have to come up on deck every hour to heave the log to see how fast the ship is going, which is generally six knots or miles.

Colmore, the sub lieutenant, is very nice; he is Senior of our mess.

Last night at 19.30 we were boiling some water to make cocoa with, and eating sardines. We boil the water by spirit lamps (methylated spirits) and there were a lot of pots of cocoa on the table and the ship suddenly gave a tremendous roll, bigger than any of the others and all the things slid off the table onto the cushions and a bottle of methylated spirits broke and caught alight on the cushions and there was a regular blaze and we all roared with laughter and hove rugs at it. Williams and I jumped on top of it and danced on it and at last it went out all except Williams lamp which was burning brightly on the deck so I stamped on it fiercely and half broke the wretched lamp and my wretched rug was thoroughly singed and saturated with cocoa and the whole concern made a horrid smell in the mess and it had to be thoroughly cleaned out and washed. It came off very luckily as it happened, because there might have been an awful row as methylated spirits are not allowed in the gun room, and besides the whole ship might have caught fire.

I don't think we are going to the Cape yet but we don't know yet *at all, at all*. Yesterday I saw a lot of black fish; they are just like whales in the distance, spouting water up into the air, and I also saw some porpoises which came first under where I was standing and I saw them quite plainly, and I expect we will soon see some dolphins chasing flying fish as the weather is rather warm. You have no idea how I'm looking forward to getting onshore at Madeira, hardly so much for seeing the place as once more to get onto terra firma, and I feel myself free again which I am far from feeling at present. There is a fellow on board, Williams, a mid who passed out of the *Britannia* with me, and we are always going about together. I like him very much. The porpoises I was telling you about jump clean out of the water about 7 feet and one of them came just under the poop. I asked him to give me one of his teeth for the letters but he did not hear me so he passed on!!! We are very squashed in the gun room; it is very small for the number of fellows and Colmore does all he can to keep it nice and clean. The food is not so bad as expected, we have a lot of preserved things.

I was not very seasick and I am very well now, not a bit sick. Sardines and things like that or drink et cetera were all called extras. You have to pay for the extra; anything we are not given is extra. We were very nearly going into Gibraltar or Lisbon because one of our pipes condensing water was smashed and we wanted it repaired, but we are not going to, however, much to my disgust, because I should have liked to have seen Gibraltar very much.

I hope you are both quite well and all the other dear ones. I think I must stop this part of my Epistle and write the next when I have something more to say. Love to all from

Your loving son, B G Godfrey Fawcett

HMS *Dido* Lat. 36. 50 N. Long 12. 59 W., Wednesday, June 25, 1879

My dearest Papa and Mother

The day after tomorrow we expect to be in Madeira. What fun it will be, I shall go for a ride and have rare jokes and won't I eat lots of fruit? Just! You can get it for next to nothing. I put the Lat and Long of our position today at noon at the top of the page. It is very hot. I don't think we have seen anything unusual since I wrote the last letter. Being Midshipman of the Watch in the day is beastly humbug. Four hours at a time and you are expected to know everything. In talking, we never use the word lie; if you want to say lie, we must say "Ananias": "He told an Ananias." We play backgammon a great deal. I like it very much. The other sub lieutenant, Lindsay by name, is also very nice, as well as Colmore. I like him very much.

9:15 pm. A sea has just come in through our gunroom port and soused us. I have got my hind quarters rather wet, and now it is being wiped up, having gone into our lockers which are just under the port. I have only got my cash box in mine. I hope you got the portmanteau all safe and that the address did not come off. I must finish in a minute. I'm so frightfully hot. Our average speed for one hour is about 5 kn, our fastest speed was 8½ kn and our lowest 1½ kn. I must go on deck now and get cool and then turn in, so good night to you both and all the other dear ones.

June 27th 1879, Friday, Madeira.

The first land we sighted was at about 11 am today; it was the island of Porto Santo, a very desolate looking large island, and then 40 miles on after that we saw Madeira and anchored off the town; on the way in we fired a salute of 21 guns to the Portuguese flag and we will have to fire 21 more tomorrow for the Queen (Coronation Day) and five for the British Consul, and we were saluted back by 21 from a feeble Portuguese fort. And we (midshipmen) have all got leave to go on shore for the whole day tomorrow. There is a place from which you slide down about a mile and I and Williams shall go on that and we shall go for a jolly ride and eat fruit. What a dreadful thing about the Prince Imperial been killed at Zululand, if it is true. I don't believe it yet though.

I am looking forward to the letters, we expect the mail[12] in tonight and then the letters will go straight home; perhaps I will be able to send you another letter before we leave Madeira. It is so awfully hot and I sweat most awfully, which is a very good sign. I'm going to turn out at 5 o'clock tomorrow

---

12 not the letters themselves, but the ship used to bring and take the letters

morning and go on shore at 5.30 and spend the day. The water is so horrible and quite hot. I drink as little as possible. I'm going to try and get some cartridges at Madeira. Please send these letters onto Granny, then I need not write again, because there is not much time. We will have to turn in soon so I think I must wind up. Give my best love to darling granny, aunts J. R. & H, Nora and Maud, Hilda and baby and Merle, Miss Hartland and all the others.

Such a pity oranges and grapes are not ripe yet! Only bananas, peaches, pears, apples, strawberries, cherries, et cetera et cetera! I daresay I will be able to buy some nice little curiosities and send them home; please send me out six drill coats and six drill trousers as soon as possible. I don't know where you can send them to, I'm sure. How is everything going on at home? I have all my gold studs and watch safe and well, the watch starts every day. There are some fellows in here with nightshirts and jerseys on. The lights are to go out now so good night –

Love to all from Your Loving Son

Brian G Godfrey-Faussett

The convent at Madeira by B G-F.

July 14, 1879 – Monday [presumed to be from Sierra Leone]

Dearest Mother

It is so frightfully hot, 81° [27°C] in the shade and on deck where there is a little wind, and it is much more down here in the gun room; it is about 93° [34°C]. I have only got trousers, jersey and shirt on. We had a tornado, a tremendous squall, lightning and thunder and rain and wind; we had to take in all our sails when it came on. We (the midshipmen) and two clerks were in the middle of our drill rifle and cutlass drill. We have been doing single stick drill or fencing lately and in the afternoon we have fencing with each other and lay in, hitting as hard as we can. I have got a lot of scars and I've also given plenty!!!

Today (Wednesday) it has been raining the whole morning and it is my forenoon watch (8.30 to 12.30) but we are working in the Captain's cabin as it is raining and we can't work in the gun room because it is to hot and too small; on fine days we have a table put just up under the poop and we work on that, but that is awfully hot. We wear white trousers and white cap covers and we are allowed to wear straw hats and so I wear one, having bought one at Madeira. Things were dear there; I gave 3 shillings and 4 pence for it; they asked 4 shillings for it. I bought a few curios (curiosities). I will tell you all about what I did at Madeira on another sheet. Don't forget please about the six white jackets and white trousers, please ask Frasers to make the trousers decently big. Do you like the crest? I don't think it is bad. Please could you get a photograph of the *Dido* for me, I would like to put it into my logbook, Groom Photographers, Queen St, Plymouth, should reach him, I should think.

Williams and myself were sent up aloft the other day for lounging about on the quarterdeck and we had to do some drill, set the royal sail and ditto the topgallant sail and the best of it was that two of the other midshipmen were sent up to help us.

I wonder what Sierra Leone is like, we are nearly in sight of land now (9 pm). I'm not quite certain about passing my exam. When you get this it will be over. You know I can't be plucked altogether, the most the Captain can do is put me back about six weeks, which some think is likely. I did not tell you that we (the gun room) had some sheep, eight, which William's father gave us, so we have not had much salt grub, which is a very good thing; we also had some chickens which we bought. It is all humbug about the officers being provided with ice. We have none. We bought two coolers at Madeira which cools the water little bit; one of the coolers is broken already. Our cooler is about 1 foot high, made of crockery.

On this next sheet of foreign paper I will tell you what I did at Madeira, for we had great fun there. Captain Sinclair is here on the *Dwarf*; he is not very well I believe and is staying at the hospital ashore. He came on board here today and asked about me but I was on shore today and looked about me. The people have such picturesque dresses on, some of the little children wear none at all. We had dinner at an hotel, not much of one certainly, still we went there to eat. Then we went and looked at a Monkey for sale for 24 shillings, a very good one, perhaps we are going to buy him and it will be great fun. We are all going to bring some parrots back with us. I have got a few curios and two photos of Madeira which I am sending to you. We arrived in here on Friday (today being Saturday) and we anchored outside here on Thursday night to wait for daylight and come in. It is a beautiful place, a simple paradise if it was not for the fever. There are some rows going on up the Gambia River so rows are expected. An old chief wants to play the fool with us because our flag is hoisted up there. Perhaps some of us will go up there but it is not likely. I daresay I'll go and see Captain Sinclair tomorrow.

I can't make out why I have not had any letters from home, if you address them HMS *Dido* West Coast of Africa they would reach me, I expect, by the next mail which comes in in two or three days. I think I will tell you all about Madeira now in the other letters.

Goodbye now, Darling.

HMS *Dido*, Freetown, Sierra Leone, July 19, 1879, Saturday Night

Dearest Papa and Mother,

At 10 we came in sight of Madeira, I came on deck and looked at everything. First we passed the most lonely looking island called Porto Santo, a most desolate looking place with very few people in it; then we got close to Madeira, when you could see heaps of plantations, vineyards et cetera. Well, we fired a salute of 21 guns in honour of the Portuguese flag and went in and anchored close to the Fort, which, by the by, feebly returned our salute.

On the following day I got leave with Williams so we went on shore and first were assailed by a man who asked us if we wanted any horses, so we told him yes, so he became our guide. First he took us to the food market where we bought some fruit, followed the whole time by a lot of dirty Portuguese then he took us to his stables where we saw two very fine-looking horses, so we bargained for about 10 minutes and then told him we would give him five shillings each to take us up to the Convent nearly up at the top of the hill, a place where everyone goes to. So we mounted our steeds and after a good deal of jumping and prancing about, we galloped them on with about four guides running after us. Well, we got up to the Convent at last and dismounted having had some beautiful views, so we paid our men for the horses and were taken into the Convent, which is just like a Roman Catholic Church, only more so; it had a lot of massive silver ornaments and also some tin ones. Well, having seen that we came out, bowing to an old priest as we passed him (we saw some people confessing in the church) and when we got out we saw two of our officers who talked to us and asked us if we were going down in the sledges, things that run right down from the Convent to the bottom of the hill at a tremendous pace, so we got on and started our downward journey; halfway down the men stopped and said they were thirsty so we gave them a penny and then they got something and we started on again and got to the bottom where we gave them three shillings each, too much as we afterwards found out.

Then we walked on and found our way to Miles Hotel, a very nice house where I spent much of my time, the whole time we were at Funchal and we told them we wanted luncheon and dinner and then went off to see if we could bathe. After we had walked along the beach under a broiling sun and frightful heat we arrived at a place which satisfied Williams but not myself. We sat down and Williams bathed while I looked on holding a loaded revolver (which Williams always carries with him) to shoot anybody that came to bag his clothes. Then we went back to Miles and had a very good luncheon and spent most of the afternoon there in the garden belonging to the Hotel and playing billiards and watching the many lizards running about. Well, the other days we spent much the same way. I came on shore every day, bought some curios; one of the best, a cap I send you, you see the old men going about Funchal in them. I had rare rows with the boatman coming off at night and day. Colmore and I ran one man into the Consul about not taking us off without paying him beforehand but he got the worst of it and had to take us off.

We then started for Sierra Leone, having been four days at Madeira and now I don't think there is much to say. One of the photos is of the convent and the other is a view of Funchal – HMS *Dido* was anchored just where that ship you see is near the Fort. And now I must dry up. I will tell you about my adventures at Freetown, Sierra Leone in some further letter.

There is a lot of ship shifting going on. I might be put into some other ship because I am only a supernumerary but there are other supers on board. I wish you would write up to the Admiralty to ask them not to change me or something like that, because you could not possibly be under nicer officers. There was a race between two of our cutters, nothing much happened except that one of them beat the other!!! I'm sending two of the *Dido* ship ribbons, you may care to have them. Now I suppose I must wish you a good night as it is rather late. I may add another line tomorrow before the mail goes. We are the senior officers in the station now, there are two other ships here now, the Dwarf and Pioneer, gunboats

from Your Loving Son

B.G. Godfrey-Faussett

(Love and kisses to all)

HMS *Dido* Freetown Sierra Leone, July 20, 1879 Tuesday night

Darling Papa and Mother

The mailbag leaves the ship tonight and then the mail starts tomorrow morning at 8 am. Pitman (the Chaplain), Williams, Igling[?] and myself are going out shooting tomorrow. Igling is the only one who has no gun. We are going to pull up at a point where we land, about 4 miles off and we begin shooting partridges, I believe the birds are. I will take care I don't pump myself, never fear. There are such beautiful butterflies here, Williams and I are going to make a collection. This is such a lovely place; yesterday Pitman, Williams and myself went for a walk and got near a large house on Plantation Place so as we were thirsty we walked calmly in, expecting that the place belongs to a Negro, but we were shown in and we walked upstairs hearing all the time some fair creature playing the piano and singing lustily and beautifully. It suddenly ceased and the old lady, a mulatto, showed us into a little boudoir affair off a large room and she sent for some cocoa and water which I did not care much about, and we all talked and soon her daughter came in, a fair dark creature. Well we talked and then the fair one, Miss Maud Rosenbush, sang and played very nicely. Then she showed us some photos and then we went out and walked about. There was a walk they called Coffee Avenue and Coconut Avenue. I have got two coffee berries and the old lady gave me the two very pretty shells which she had picked up. Tell Laura they will make a very nice addition to our collection and the old lady (not the *young* one, mind) kindly made me plant a little rosebush because she said she could remember me by it!!! After they had crowded us with flowers we came away came on board in the evening. The people wear such very picturesque dresses. If I can I will get some photos and send them to you. I hope you send the letters to Granny and the others.

Goodbye now, Darling Papa and Mother, give my best love to the other ones.

From your loving son
BG Godfrey-Faussett

HMS *Dido*, Freetown, Sierra Leone, Saturday, July 20, 1879

Dearest Papa and Mother,

I have passed my seamanship exam yesterday and did part of my study exam, and my instruments were examined today. I think I shall pass all right; the First Lieutenant and Second and Third Lieutenants examined me, Messrs Michaelson, Charters and Ogle, they were very nice and today when my instruments were examined, my telescope, sextant and instruments, they were all very clean.

I'm writing this letter in the wardroom because our gun room is being cleaned out so the doctor (Dr Atkinson), who I like very much, has asked me to come and write my letters in here. I will now tell you about my shooting expedition. We (Colmore), Mr. Pitman (Naval Instructor) Williams and myself started at 4.30 on the morning and went on shore with our guns. I had my plain clothes on with canvas gaiters on my legs and my gun and went on shore and walked 5 miles, five blessed miles!, to the lighthouse; on the way we had a few shots at some quail and wild ducks, but I did not have a shot!!! Then we went over a ferry in a very shaky kind of boat, a canoe (very long) shape out of a tree and walked on till we came to the lighthouse, passing a lot of natives dressed very funnily and some with hardly any dresses on at all!!! Well, when we came to the lighthouse we opened out and commenced walking through grass and stuff up to your neck. I got the first shot at a bird, a large one about the size of a pheasant. I waited till he flew off a coconut tree and then I had a shot at him and wounded him but I could not go after him in the long grass so we passed on and separated. I tumbled down into a small hollow as I was walking along. Well, I walked all over the place, met one or two of the others and separated again. I rose a brace of partridges (the game we had come out for) but could not get a shot at them as they flew so low and got hid behind bushes; then I came back towards the lighthouse (raining nearly the whole time) and shot three birds and wounded a magpie. I send you the wings of two of them, if they do not smell too much when I come to put them in the envelope. One of them was a beautiful blue bird with a long beak and short tail; the beak is black on the top and red underneath. The other is a yellow bird. I chased them a long time without being able to get any and the other was a stupid brown bird about as big as a thrush. Then I began to go towards home and found Colmore and our guide looking for me. They had all had breakfast about a mile from where I was and I thought I had lost myself or been bitten by a snake or something like that so I went back with my spoils to the natives' house, but I had some breakfast and drank some rum to prevent myself from getting the fever and then we started back to walk home and arrived on board at about 2 pm, where I changed and had a bath and saw Captain St Clair and talked to him.

HMS *Dido*, July 27 Sunday, Freetown, Sierra Leone.

Dearest Mother and Papa

I must now tell you about my adventures with Captain St Clair. First I must tell you that your letter and Curteis's and Dico's were hailed with great glee by me that evening. Well, the other night we had theatricals on board, performed by some of our blue jackets,[13] it was not bad, and I and another midshipman, Dawney, dined in the gun room. All of us could not dine there because there were some guests off the other two ships, Sub Lt Tuck, Lt Seymour and a doctor and Colmore and Lindsay, our two subs. Well, after dinner we smoked and looked at the theatricals and I saw Captain St Clair, so I went and spoke to him and he gave me a cigarette and he asked after all of you, and asked me to go out for a walk with him the next afternoon and have dinner with him, so next day he called for me in his gig at 4 o'clock and we went on shore and first we went to His Excellency the Governor in Chief of Sierra Leone and we talked to him and he gave me iced lemon and soda. This was very good and the first cold stuff I have drunk or tasted since I had left England. When we went away he told me that I might go up there and take somebody else with me to have more iced lemon and soda, but I won't be, as he is not considered a nice man. Then we went up to the barracks and I was introduced to the officers and we listened to the band playing, and then we went into the mess and talked and went and looked at the officer's quarters; they have heaps of room. The Regiment is a West India one. Then we went down and I was in plain clothes and I had no time to change which was very dreadful as there was our First Lt. and Lindsay and the First Lt. of the *Dwarf*, Captain St Clair's ship. Well, I put on one of Captain St. C.'s white jackets which was like a sack on my shoulders. After dinner they played whist and I looked on and then Lt Archdale, First of the *Dwarf* showed me a lot of photos of the Mediterranean. Then we came on board the *Dido* again and turned in.

Yesterday (Sunday) we, Williams, Miall (Assistant Clerk) and myself went out and Williams took a small bulldog revolver and Miall took a kind of gun

---

13 naval ratings /enlisted men

like a pistol that turns into a stick and that about once in eight times goes off. Well, we shot nothing but I knocked over a very small bird by heaving my stick at it; I send you its wings. We lost ourselves once and after wandering about we came upon an old native's hut, where we had to give him two shillings, having nothing less, for eight coconuts for the sake of the milk; a man swarmed up the tree to get them. I have had dinner once in the wardroom, the officers are very jolly to me. Mr Michaelson, Number One (which means First Lt) showed me the letter he had sent him asking him to look after me. I have not yet received any letters or newspapers from you before yesterday so all the others must have gone to the Cape; you should address merely:- HMS *Dido*, West Coast of Africa Station (or elsewhere). If I go to the Cape then you must address to the Cape.

HMS *Tandos*[?] came in this morning, she looks such a jolly ship; she is bigger than us, and is painted black. The mail starts in about one hour. I believe I am now going to read mummy's letter and write by it. Thanks for the photo of the Prince Imperial. I like it very much. What a sad thing it was about his death. What fun about you and the Seamen's Mission.

It has done nothing but rain here except for the last two or three days. How nice Fred Roberts being made KCB. Thanks for sending the photo of *Dido*, the trousers, flowers et cetera. How nice the greenhouse must be. How is Maud getting on with her fiddle? I am quite well now. The mailbag is just going I believe. I believe I have passed my exam, love to all the darling ones your loving son,

B G Godfrey-Faussett.

Freetown, Sierra Leone, August 2nd 1879, Saturday

Dear Dico,

Thanks very much for your nice letter and Curteis's. I wonder how you would like being here, not very much, I expect. We have got a monkey on board and he bears a decided likeness to my brother and he is always making a row. We are going to buy a young leopard, or Colmore is I believe, to have him on board as a pet: they will cut his teeth out I suspect, because he will be biting when he grows older probably, and we have also on board a black tomcat. Everything is so damp: this paper which I have kept in my chest is quite damp, all my books are perfectly white with mildew and we will have cockroaches on board soon, which will be frightful, so I shall kill all I can. There is a place on shore which I believe was intended for a church in which is in ruins now and darkish inside and the place is crammed full of bats; some of the fellows have been there and shot some with walking stick pistols. Yesterday the doctor and the Chaplain went there and saw a large white owl and they tried hard to get it but it got behind a beam. I think I shall go on shore with my gun and try to shoot it.

I hope you are getting on well at College and that you have got into the second side. You will be at home for the holidays when you get this. The outward and homeward mail steamers came into harbour today (Saturday) and I don't know when the homeward bound one goes, so I must be quick with my letters. Tell Curteis I liked his letter very much and that I will write to him soon. What side is Curtis on? I have just received three nice letters from Papa, Nora and Maud. I expect you will play lots of tennis in the square. Now I must say goodbye because I have to write to papa and mother. Write again as soon as you like I don't mind how many letters you send me.

HMS *Dido*, Freetown, Sierra Leone, August 3, 1879 Sunday

I hope my letters telling you how to address my letters have reached you. I got the letter from you, Papa, enclosing one from Nora and Maud and addressed to the Cape, and your letter, Mother, must have gone on to the Cape. There is a mail that goes straight to the Cape and another that touches at Madeira, Sierra Leone and Cape Coast Castle from which place it comes home again so all my letters have gone to the Cape except two or three which by chance I got. I am so much obliged to Nora and Maud for their nice letters. I was lying in a grass hammock just outside the gun room reading theirs and Papa's. I hope Mama and Papa and the two babes enjoyed themselves at Sherborne. I wish there were strawberries out here. I have finished and passed my exam, it was harder and more things to do than I expected. I send you my marks: I hope you will be pretty well satisfied. If I had not been at home for so long I am certain (or very nearly certain) that I could have passed first-class instead of third …

I had a nice letter from Dico and another from Curteis by the last mail. It certainly is very sad about the death of the Prince Imperial but it will be more sad I think if Lt Carey gets punished in any way. All the officers on board think is a great shame the way they are going on about it. It is very nice General Roberts having been made a KCB. How glad Lady Roberts must be!

I think I will be able to pick up a few curiosities. I have got one or two already, the old Cap I sent you home is one. Do send me photos of the ship. I wish (as the ship is not going to the Cape until after the war is nearly over) that I had got some other ship. I like all the officers very well but it is such a rotten station, so hot. If we were going to the seat of war it would be all right but we won't go there, we think, for about two months.. There is a fellow on board, who is in a dreadful way because he has not come out here thinking he was going to the war, it was a regular sell for everyone.

Send me some of my photos, mother, please if you have any to spare you know the kind I like, the one leaning, not the one standing up straight. I hope Miss H. is better for her being at Ilfracombe. At present the sweat is rolling all down my neck and everywhere although the two ports are open also the two doors and we burn only one lamp it is dreadful weather for clean clothes: they charge 3/- a day to wash your clothes and then they tear and pull them apart and you have to put on a clean shirt every other day, sometimes more. I have got very little money left. This is winter so I am afraid the summer will suffocate me. I wish you would try and send me some of this kind of foreign paper because I can hardly write on the other sort with a sharp pen and when I have written you can hardly read it because the ink all shows through. They are getting awfully strict, we have to keep night watches in harbour now and we never used to keep watch at all in harbour.

I dined in the wardroom again the other night. I don't know if I told you but I have such a delicious servant, an Irishman he is such fun and he makes a very good servant. I am having a piece of the lining taken out of my tailcoat to make my midshipman's patches with. I feel much bigger now that I am a mid. I shall be an acting sub-Lt when I am on the way home. We are going to have a young leopard on board I believe. It was such fun in church today. Our monkey came in and sat in front on the deck, walked about and then sat down again and looked up into the bosun's face and looked very comical and squeaked and made us all laugh. Whenever the mail is sighted from the lookout station, a shore gun is fired so we all appear on deck highly anxious to see if it is the outward or homeward bound mail. I have not exchanged any of my things but I tried to exchange mother's big silver chain with a native for a grass hammock or two and a place mat but he would not!!! I will be able to do it better when we get further south. How is Mr Vibart? I hope he is better. Maud was telling me in her letters about some man who killed a woman, but I never got the letter which told me the beginning and part of it I expect it went on to the Zulus!!! Give Miss H. my love. I have nothing more to say and Lindsay is persuading me to stop saying I have written quite enough. so goodbye much love to all.

HMS *Dido*, Sierra Leone, August 10, 1879 Sunday

I don't think there is much news this time to tell you. I wore my Mid's patch today properly for the first time. Captain Wright asked me to dine with him the other night and I wore it then, that is the only time. I don't know how much longer we are going to remain in this place. I am getting rather tired of it. I have not been onshore much lately. I am about the only fellow in the gun room except the subs and the Clerk and Assistant Clerk that has not been seedy yet at all. Four of the fellows have been seedy, one of them, Nicholson, had a slight touch of the fever and although I went out shooting that day and got wet through, really I never felt anything, not even a cold.

We have got four monkeys on board and probably will soon have some parrots; one of the monkeys belongs to Colmore and as he and Williams are away on a shooting expedition about 10 miles inland, I am looking after his monkey for him; it is a very nice little fellow although he nips you now and then. I feed him on fruit and I am going to get one I think, you could get a good one for 2/6 but I don't think I shall because they make such a mess. If I do, you need not be afraid of my bringing it home because it is sure to die before we pay off. I believe we are going to have a young leopard on board. I was saying that Colmore and Williams went out on an expedition 10 miles inland. Well, they started Friday morning at 5 o'clock and it was my morning watch, I saw them start. They are coming back today or are supposed to do so. They have gone to look for big game, leopards, deer jackals et cetera. They hope to get a leopard or two if they can because there are some about. Colmore told me that if he found there was good shooting to be had he would take me there for some days, it will be such monstrous fun, fancy getting a leopard!. The night before they started I was helping them to make their Cartridges with bullets and buckshot. Williams took his revolver with him and they took heaps of grub and a Krooman to carry the bag. They also took what we call army suits, that is a suit made out of common blankets to sleep in, I shall take one if I go. I am longing for them to come back for Williams to tell me all about it. The other day I went up with Chappell (the Clerk) to bathe in the baths belonging to the offices at the barracks. Chappell lets me write my letters in the office sometimes. I like him. The other day when the *Tenedos* came in (she has left for somewhere) she bought a great turtle with her which we took on board; the poor brute was put on its back and there it was lying on the deck miserable – it was an enormous beast and weighed heaps of hundredweight's. The *Tenedos* was exactly the same size as us but she is painted black and we are white. I believe we are going to be painted black soon. Don't make any more mistakes about my address, simply HMS *Dido*, West Coast of Africa station (or elsewhere). If I am at the Cape of course you must address to me there.

On Monday I think I will go out shooting cockyollie birds et cetera. Was it not that wing I sent you a very pretty one? I knocked a bird over with my stick last Sunday, it was very small and there were a lot of them together!!! I have had a lot of rows with the native washerwoman here. I gave my washing to one at the rate of three shillings a dozen, and when she came on board I paid her having bargained with her a good deal, just at the rate of two shillings a dozen. Then when she was looking into the mess Colmore came down and shoved her shawl or something over her head. Somebody else tied a piece of string round it and then her head was bottled!!! Her name is Miss Roseanne Williams; well then she got simply furious and walked about, tearing nearly all her clothes off her and told the officers et cetera. At last she went away taking some more of my clothes with her to be washed; about two days afterwards the skipper got a letter saying something about *'one Godfrey-Faussett did unlawfully and wilfully strike and inflict stripes upon her'* or something like that and she also said I did not pay her money. Well, anyhow, the skipper cares not and I care not, and now I hope she will soon bring back my washing; but having had a letter from Rosanna Williams I was prepared for her and she said she will go up to the skipper too.

We are going to have a concert on board on Tuesday. I suppose it will be exactly the same as it has been before. Today I went onshore and bathed at the barrack baths with Chapell. Colmore and Williams have come back. They only got two wild pigs and a couple of brace of partridges and wounded a big deer which they followed by his blood for some way but at last he got into a thick jungle so they gave up the chase; they had a very good house to sleep in and are both looking better than when they left. They say it is wonderfully cool up there and they took their quinine every day!!! I shall have to go on watch soon so I must finish my letter tomorrow. The homeward bound mail has just come in, the mail from England is expected on Tuesday. We are going to have a cricket match I believe soon. Fancy, we have been here about four blessed weeks and the Admiralty regulations are that no ship shall stay here more than three days because it is unhealthy. I have not felt anything the matter with my heart since I left England. It has been raining nearly the whole morning, such weather! On the whole it is rather good weather for the rainy season. They have been firing our field gun all the forenoon at a target and they have not hit it yet. Now I really must go. I really don't have anything more to say. I hope I shall get lot of nice letters when the mail comes in. Give my best love to Papa and all the others. Remember me to Nurse and I hope Miss H is well again.

HMS *Dido*, Sierra Leone, August 18, 1879, Monday

The mail goes about 12 o'clock I believe so I must be quick and write. We played the garrison here the other day at cricket and we beat them. We are going to play them again today. I have not played in the match, I'm sorry to say, as it is going to be sent to *The Field*. I went out shooting on Saturday and shot a vulture or kite or some big bird, a scavenger, and I was asked by the natives not to shoot any more as they eat all the dirt, and I also shot a magnificent owl in an old Church. I brought it on board and gave it to one of the officers who tried to skin it but failed so he kept a wing. I would much rather have kept it myself and sent the wings home. They would have made a beautiful fan. There are two more so I shall go and try and shoot them tomorrow. I also shot a lot of hideous big bats. The cartridges here are an awful price, a guinea a hundred. I lunched in the gunroom yesterday.

I'm so glad that you, mother, and darling May Bee enjoyed yourselves at Sherborne I'm sure Hilda and you Papa enjoyed yourselves too. Aunt Emy has not written to me yet. I hope you and Papa will have a photo taken soon and send me one. You have not sent me one of Dico yet. I have not received any papers, they all go to the Cape because you address them wrong; you can send me as many as you don't want. I'm going to copy some out of the *Sp and D News*[14] soon. I have not received the parcel yet either, that has also gone to the Cape. The heat at present is enough to drive you mad, so what it will be like farther south! Besides, this is the coolest part of the year … We are going away from here soon, we are waiting anxiously for the mail from home, expecting to sight it at any minute. I hope it has orders for us to go directly to the Cape. I'm so sorry about poor little Rose.

We had another concert the other day, the worst of all and the governor came on board. Captain St Clair went up the river the other day for three or four days and got seven guineas a day for being in command. The *Firefly* will meet us soon, so I suppose as I shall see Curteis. What a shame about Carey. Most awful excitement, one of the mids just came down, about 20 minutes ago, in a state of excitement to say that a large canoe had capsized and the natives were floating in the water so I rushed up and saw about 30 natives floating and swimming in the water, and two bullocks with a man hanging onto one of them. All this took place away from the shore, about 400 yards from us, so we lowered all our remaining boats and sent them to the scene. I wish I could have got away on a boat. Now I must go up and see what they are doing. There were some women there, I don't know if they were all saved or

---

14 *Sporting & Dramatic News*

not. They are landing all the natives.

Our skipper is very ill, I expect he will be invalided soon and then I don't know who will we will get. Send my love to Miss H and Nurse and now goodbye all. I will try and shoot some pretty birds so that I may send you their wings. It is a beautiful day for the cricket, I hope we will beat them again. I must stop now goodbye, much love they have just cleared the lower deck.

HMS *Dido*, August 26, 1879 Monday

I will just say I am all right and now I will go on writing with your letter by my side then I will proceed to tell you the news. What a pity that you should have addressed the letter wrong. I have received some of them. I'm glad you like the budget[?] that I sent you with the cap et cetera. I see in your letter that you are going to write to Admiral Hood for my staying in the *Dido*. I hope you have not done so because I am in no violent hurry to stay in here as you will see by one of my letters. I shall look forward to the photo of the *Dido*; by the time you get this letter I will have got the photo. How nice for Nora and Maud to be going to Rockenham. I wish I was there!! I hope Papa will go somewhere for a holiday – Norway or some nice place. I am afraid this place is not healthy enough besides there is not much fun to be had here …! I don't care about lime juice much. I wish I did.

And now I think I may tell you about the death and funeral et cetera. I was sleeping outside the Captain's on the deck, when I woke up and got up to come down and turn in as it was getting daylight. This was at 4.30 in the morning, when the sentry stopped me and told me that the Captain was dead, so I was very sorry of course. I came down and told one or two of the others, and then turned in and got to sleep. At 6.30 I turned out, of course all the talk was about the late skipper and everybody was very sorry, so at about 8.30 we hoisted out our steam cutter and launch to take him onshore and about then we were doing what we call drooping yards, when a poor blue jacket fell overboard, a very good man too; first he fell onto the main yard out of the top, then onto the nettings and then overboard. Then three men jumped overboard after him and brought him on board insensible and with his skull opened, and he died at 10.30. So in the afternoon we all put on our dress or tail coats and went onshore to the funeral, only about six men being left on board with one officer. So we started on our funeral procession with all our Marines, blue jackets, and blue jackets of the other two ships in the harbour, and the soldiers from the barracks, and the band playing, and buried them (but I must stop now and give you a full account some future time). The *Firefly* has arrived today and I went on board to lunch with Curteis. Love to all dear ones if the mail does not go so soon I will add another line, I have lots to tell you in my next letter.

HMS *Dido*, Sierra Leone, August 29, 1879

My last letter was written in a great hurry because the mail was going so soon and then it was postponed until for about two hours, which was at 9 o'clock, so I took the mailbags on board and got Captain St Clair's letters which were still in the bag and then I went and took them on board the mail boat. There was a blessed great swell on the whole time, so it was not most awfully pleasant. Having delivered the bags up to the Captain of the Mail I got receipts for them and came on board again. Captain St Clair has come on board and is acting Captain on board this ship until we get another Captain, which won't be I suppose for five or six months to come; it is very nice having Capt St Clair. Colmore has gone on board the *Daisy* as acting Lt, it is a great thing for him but we are all so sorry he has gone, he was awfully jolly. The other day I went out shooting with another fellow who brought a pistol stick with him and we started at 1130 and landed at a point near the ship and began walking along looking for partridges but found none the whole day. We shot about six cockyollie birds as we were going along Miall, the fellow I was with, drew my attention to a cat which came out of the bush and went along over some gravel heaps and he said to me "Shoot", but I could not see the beast and I thought if I did not see it I could not shoot it because it might be tame, so we went on and we saw it once more but I did not want to shoot it till it had gone; it was a large yellow cat, it might possibly have been wild but I don't think it was; it ran away stealthily into the bush. Well we went on winding our way about through the bush and at last we were going down a path, on one side, in a small tree, Miall pointed out a grass snake, one of those little brutes that are deadly poison, so this little beast was winding its way about the tree awfully fast so I waited till it stopped and then shot at it which made him hop about much more so then I had another shot at him and brought him down, the hindmost and uninteresting half of it. It is a very long and thick snake. So then we came on our way back and when we were just at the beginning of the town we met a black chap who said if we came into his place we would be able to shoot pigeons as they came to feed. 'But,' he said, 'you must be patient, very patient,' and he said he had a grass hammock and we could wait in it, but we thought that sounded like not seeing any or having to wait all night before we saw anything so we did not go in, and then a black chap came along and said if we went with him he would we would get something. I forgot to tell you that before we came across these black chaps we saw the yellow cat again, he was some way off but we were afraid he would run away so I fired at him; I hit him and he rolled over a little and then ran on into the bush. Miall's I don't expect carried so far or perhaps he might have killed him, and if we had we would have skinned him. Well, I left off when the second black chap told us we would get something if he went with him so we went on, he had a big muzzle loading gun and the first thing we saw was a large bird with a white breast flying along. I was just going to shoot him but the black chap told me not to fire at him but to wait; the old ass thought it would settle I suppose, so he got away. Well, we went on, he shot a jungle crow I shot a few cockyollie birds and that was all and then we went back and got rid of the man, then went into the old church to look for some more owls but we saw none so shot about 13 bats and then we went to Carl Boyles[?], a big grocer here, and had a lot of scalding cocoa, which burnt my tongue, and biscuits and then we came on board. Before we came on board I shot a very pretty bird and gave it to the Chaplain, Mr Pitman who collects these nice little birds. Well, I gave it to him in the boat. We were not quite sure if it was dead or not so we killed it, or thought we had so he was taken on board by the chaplain and next morning I was told by the doctor that the bird had revived in the night and sat up on his pillow and this put the chaplain in a tremendous funk and he threw it overboard!!!

And now I will tell you about the funeral and death of these two poor men, Capt Wright and L.S. Creed, a leading seaman. I woke up having been sleeping outside the Captain's door and I was told by the Sentry that the Captain was dead. This was at 4.30 and he died at 4.20. I could hardly believe it at first so I went down, told one or two others and turned in. Well the talk in the morning was of nothing else at all and at 8.30 we were drooping our yards because of his death and a poor fellow fell from the top and then onto the main yard and then onto the nettings and then overboard, insensible well, three blue jackets jumped overboard, one of them the head Krooman. He was bought on board insensible and taken down below and died at 10.30. The boats were put out and we all wore our tail coats and the funeral procession was very grand. The soldiers from the barracks and the band came, and the blue jackets on the other ships. When we buried them two stupid washerwomen made an awful row howling away pretending they were sorry and all that.

So we came on board and I am sorry to say everything is the same as before. I should be much obliged if you could send me some cash, I have not got a farthing, and our monthly pay all goes on mess extras and paying for furnishing the mess and the washing is so expensive; I have not got enough money to pay my washing. Fancy 3d. each for each single thing and the sock

3d., a pair of socks 6d. I shall have to borrow some money to pay it. I have kept as low as possible in my extras this month, about half as much as last month. The fellows who go out shooting and can get nothing else, shoot a hen and bring it back with them. They are much better than the ones they get in town. I don't know if I told you about my chest? Well, it used to be in a very nasty place, near the tank where all the blue jackets go and get water, but now that Colmore has gone I have shifted into his place. He won't come back for some time. It will be awful fun when we get to St Helena, it is a very nice place I believe.

Whenever I go ashore I generally go up to the baths and have a delicious bathe there and stay in about an hour. In the morning on board we bath behind a screen, which is rigged up on the upper deck so that we can make as much mess as we like. A few nights ago I dined with the skipper, Capt St. Clair. Curteis was there and the Governor and Secretary and our First Lieutenant and the Commander of the *Firefly*. I smoked three cigarettes. The First Lt is very nice to me. We will be crossing the line soon, I expect, it will be great fun. I have got charge of the field gun now because Lindsay who was the officer of it has taken Colmore's place so I am the "officer of the field gun" and have to drill them with the gunners mate. When we go to sea we are going to be made officers of the day watches. I have not changed my mind about getting out of the ship, I should like very much to get out of it. There is a rumour about our going to Cape Coast Castle on urgent business. We have got a kind of mess paper. We send in our submissions to the Editor, who is one of the mids, and then if the thing is worth putting in it is written into a book and if it is a drawing or a sketch to stick in. I have sent in one drawing. You make up poetry or riddles or anything cutting one another, only nothing personal is allowed. The paper comes out every Sunday; tomorrow (Sunday) I think I shall go and bathe at the barracks. I am bothered if I can think of anything else to say. Much love to all, you darling ones.

HMS *Dido* Sierra Leone, September 6, 1879, Saturday

The homeward bound mail has come in and goes out in about one hour so I have not much time for a long letter. I think the one I sent you last time was very long. Thanks so much for the photo of *Dido*. I don't think it does it credit; there was a photo taken at Portsmouth that was better than the Plymouth one I believe. We go to sea on Tuesday. I will leave a letter behind me to go by the next mail and then the next place we shall be at will be Cape Coast Castle. It makes a lot of difference whether you address a letter to the Cape or Coast because different mails take different letters. I have just written to dear

Granny, they seem to have had a bad year for getting the hay in. I hope you, Papa, still go to Norway, it will do you good, I am sure. I haven't yet had a letter from Cousin Cecil. I got a delicious letter from Granny last mail and also from Nora, from Rockingham. I have got a very nice grass hammock, I bought it about a month ago. How nice about dear little May B. and the squashed chocolate. An expedition made up of Captain St Clair, our First Lieutenant, the doctor, Atkinson and Lindsay and 17 Crew men, one engine room Artificer, a Stoker and the coxswain of the steam cutter went up the river here the other day. Our steam cutter and the governor's steam launch took them up – they went up to have an interview with some black kings, but the black kings all skedaddle and when they came in sight. They saw three alligators, I think it was, and fired at them with rifles but could not kill them. There are no stamps procurable as you will see by what is written outside on the envelope, if I had known the mail was going so soon I would have sent onshore for some; if I can get some before I post this letter I will put them on. I had a splendid bathe yesterday at the barracks baths and today I lent my gun to a fellow because it was my day on I could not go onshore. It is a bad place to lend your gun. I have caught a slight cold in my head but it is nothing much I only got it when I woke up and I intend to take care of myself so you need not be alarmed!! And if it is not gone by tomorrow I shall go to the sick bay and get a dose. One of the blue jackets favourite monkeys fell overboard this morning so they went after him in the dinghy.; he swims beautifully and looked very like a drowned rat when he came on board … Again, if any of them go overboard at sea they cannot very well be picked up so they will be drowned, there are too many in the ship already so it won't be mourned much as far as the offices are concerned. All the money I possess amounts to about two shillings. I am in debt towards my servant. I owe 10 shillings wages, 17 shillings he paid for my washing, 10 shillings he lent me to pay off some of my mess debts and he will have to pay some more if any other washing comes off. I hope you won't either of you be angry at this for two or three of the fellows are in just the same box. Now I must wind up. Love to all dear ones.

HMS *Dido*, Sierra Leone, September 7, 1879

This will be the last letter that you will get from me from Sierra Leone. I'm going to leave this letter with others which will be sent by the next mail. We go to sea on Tuesday. The mail from England came in today (Sunday) and brought me three letters and a paper. I get got a letter from Papa, Maisey and cousin Cecil. By the by, don't send me any more *Sporting and Gun News*, because we take it in. I hope you, Papa, had lots of fun and good luck in Norway. Mind you write and tell me all about it. I hope you had a good passage to and fro. I suppose you are not able to bring the fish from Norway to England, though they should last much longer than out here. We had to bury poor Captain Wright and Creed's bodies the same day they died and even six hours after Creed died they had to bring his body out of the sick bay onto the upper deck because it was beginning to smell. I saw both the bodies I went in and saw the captain's cabin and looked at him. He looked very calm. We got another turtle on board the other day from "Active" and last night we had some very good turtle soup. Cousin Cecil seems to be having a pretty jolly time of it going about. I'm so glad to hear that you, mother, were going over to Rockenham, it is so long since you were there. I don't know that he has much to thank you for my kindness because I did not do much. I should like some of the paper you, mother, spoke to me about and what you wrote on. I shall like to think of you wearing my wing in one of your caps. I'm not very brown, of course I am a little, and I should be much more so after a bit. Dico sent me a very nice letter by this mail, and tell him if he was near enough I would kiss him!!! What fun it must have been his bolstering the unfortunate dormitory master. I should advise you, Dico, to take my racket back to college with you.

The choir which is composed of a few blue jackets and Marines is at present croaking away on the poop. We are going to get a brass band out from England I believe. I'm better today (Sunday), in my last letter I told you I had a cold in my head, well I am better today and it will be all gone tomorrow. All the letters I get I put in the pocket dodge [?] you gave me, mother, and every now and then I read some of them over. I'm just going to have a cup of tea. We have extra tea, 2d. per cup every night at 9 o'clock. I shall be very glad when we leave this place for we have been here so long Cousin Cecil sent me a very long letter this mail … I think I shall turn in now as it is my middle watch and in case I'm unable to add another line before we sail for Cape Palmas. Goodbye, Love to all dear ones

HMS *Dido* Sierra Leone, September 9, 1879

I am afraid I have not got much to say this time – we go to sea this afternoon in about four hours, at 4.30. I am very glad we're going to call at Cape Palmas on the way down, where there is a lot of shooting I believe. I am quite well today and this morning I went onshore for the last time and had a delicious bathe for only about half an hour. Number One (otherwise the First Lieutenant) has made our pinnace look so jolly, he has scraped the white paint off the top of it and varnished and polished it instead. There is also a kind of badge with *Dido* on it on each side of the bows outside. He intends making a lot of improvements to the ship … The canoes that go about here are such funny little things. They're simply hollowed out of a tree, very thin, the men inside being naked all except for a bit of cloth or something tied round their waists. I will send you one or two small sketches soon of this place. I'm going to try and paint a picture of the *Dido*. But I am wandering on, the mail will soon be closed so goodbye to all dear ones till I get to Cape Palmas.

HMS *Dido*, Monday, September 15, 1879

I have not much to say to you except that I am quite well. We are at present off Cape Palmas, we arrived here last night and anchored very near to a reef, where the waves are dashing fiercely; we are going out this evening en route for Cape Coast Castle. There is a large mail steamer up on the beach with the waves dashing against her; she's been there 4 years, she is made of iron therefore she is able to stand the waves. Last night one of the officers tried to land in our cutter but came out because of the breakers. There are lots of sharks about here. I hope you will excuse my writing in pencil, but it is my afternoon watch and the mail goes at about 4 o'clock. I am writing this lying on the deck on a flag and am now looking at the steamer on the sand and the waves breaking all over her or rather splashing over her. One of the fellows is fishing over the stern for an enormous fish we have seen coming up to the reef, about 1½ yards long.

I very often haul out my photo book and look at the photos of you all. I wish you, Papa, would have one taken, and I should like one of you, Mother, in your new dress. And now I must dry up because it is so hot and I shall go to sleep. One thing you will be glad of is that at sea now we don't keep night watches, only morning and day watches, but instead of keeping them, we turn out at 5:30pm for drill till 8 o'clock and then we have to keep watches. And now I must just crawl down and address an envelope. I can get no stamps, nobody is going or has been onshore. I shall write you a long letter when we get to Cape Coast Castle. You cannot see to read or write in the gun room it is pitch dark; much love to all.

HMS *Dido*, Cape Coast Castle, September 21, 1879

First and foremost I will just tell you this, that you had better send a letter by the 17th October mail leaving England, to catch the ship at St Helena otherwise I won't get one there from you, and also to Ascension by mail leaving England 7th November, and now for some news.

Last time I wrote to you all lying off Cape Palmas and wrote in pencil and now we are at Cape Coast Castle; it is not a bad sort of place but worse than Sierra Leone! Yesterday I went onshore and looked about with another chap Well, we got on shore and were followed by a lot of natives, four in number. They would not go away. We walked along the beach looking at the breakers and we suddenly came across a cow just dying. A lot of natives had just been bullying it. Well, it did not smell nice so we went on and passed by a big salt lagoon where there were some young natives fishing for small fish. Then after our dreary walk in which there was nothing interesting enough to relate, we went down and sat on a rock, having two hours to wait for a boat in front of the barracks. One of the officers, after looking at us through a telescope, came down and asked me to go up and have something so I called Miall who was chasing birds … [Remainder of letter unfinished]

HMS *Dido*, Accra, Gold Coast, September 25, 1879

Please thank Aunt Julia for the photo of Sir Walter, I like it very much indeed. I will write to her by next mail. This morning we mids and clerks et cetera and all those who had chests had had them up on deck and we took all our gear out and everything. I hung my clothes upon a line on the poop and hauled all my linen et cetera out and aired everything. I have a large bag full of dirty things and all at the rate of 3d. each piece, my washing bill will be something enormous. My boots are in an awful state, all mouldy, and Martin (that's my servant) brushed them and wiped them so now they are a little better. But they are all shapes and sizes and will be very uncomfortable. You have no idea how mouldy everything gets, all my collars are a little mouldy because a drop of water happened to get into my file … We are going to St Helena soon and when we get there we are all sent out of the ship ashore and live at an hotel for four or five days. Well that is really most awful fun … When we were leaving Cape Coast Castle we left under sail, the steam was not up and there was also a very strong current and we nearly ran into a merchant ship. It was such awful excitement because it was all left to the sails, we could not do anything, and the wind and helm. I was on the poop with the First Lieutenant and saw it all. We nearly anchored again, but we did not, so we proceeded on our way and anchored that evening on the coast somewhere about a mile off the land, which has no name so I cannot tell you where it was, but we were afraid to proceed at night because we were too near the land, and then the next morning we proceeded and in the evening (last evening) we arrived in this place, Accra. We will proceed tomorrow probably to Lagos anchoring the same as before the evening and then on to Quitta or some such place. I expect to find my clothes that you sent out, then we will go down the coast and then cut across to St Helena and Ascension. We will stay about three weeks at St Helena. Lagos is a place where there are hundreds of sharks. We are going to blow up a 100lb. torpedo there, attracting the sharks towards the place first by a piece of pork, it will be great fun. We hope to kill a lot of sharks that way, besides catching them on hooks.

We had a hook out all last night with a piece of pork on it but we have caught nothing. I hope you are flourishing at home Mind you, Papa, to write to me and tell me all about your excursion to Norway. Last, on a homeward bound [ship] we invalided our Paymaster and a blue jacket. I should like to go home too!! And now I think I must stop as the mail goes soon so just to wind up, telling you I am quite well. Love to all

HMS *Dido* off Quitta, Sunday, September 25, 1879

I have just written a letter to Aunt Julia in which I have asked her for her photo and thanked her. We are at present anchored of Quitta. There are only a few huts and a custom house here, and I am afraid that they have not got my parcel after all. Today Colmore's monkey fell overboard, a mid called Bruce was chasing him up aloft and the monkey made a jump from the mizzen rigging onto the cross Jack yard and slipped, I suppose, anyhow he fell overboard. At first we did not know what it was but thought it was a bottle. I was on the poop. Because it fell so heavily it did not come to the top of the water for some time but at last he came up and commenced swimming. Well, we at once hove to and lowered the lifeboat and searched for him for about one hour but could not see the poor little fellow. I suppose he must have been gobbled up by some foul shark, so now we have only two monkeys on board and a black cat. We also have a goat or African sheep on board which was brought by a Krooman who joined us at Cape Palmas. The last time I wrote to you was from Accra. I did not land there and I don't expect I will land here either. The natives here are very nearly naked, they come off to the ship in canoes and some come in a surf boat or big kind of broad boat with bows at each end. When they were bringing anybody off, they sing and make a great row. I like this paper very much. The writing does not show through like it does on the other … We have not heard of the *Dwarf* for some time, she is evidently trying to keep clear of us because we are the senior officers. I told you in my last letter about the day we left Cape Coast Castle and nearly ran into a barge. It is so dreadfully hot, 79° [26°C] in the shade, but it will be much hotter than that soon. I don't know what kind of a joke we are going to have when we cross the line. The first lieutenant, Mr Michaelson, has been kind enough to keep my photo and book in his cabin because it gets all mouldy and spoiled if I keep it in my chest or locker. I wish I had another of you, Mother, you Papa and Dico. You have not sent me any of Dico yet or of myself. You know the kind I am likely to want, not the one standing upright. The mail probably goes away tomorrow so I may be able to put another line in … This is the worst possible station in the world. You see less on this station than any other, in fact the only things you do see are palm trees, huts, natives and sand, and you are frightfully hot all day long and have every chance of catching the fever, but you might like to know that I am perfectly well and now good night and love to both of you and all the other dear ones.

HMS *Dido*, September 29, 1879

There is not much to say. I have just sent you the wing of a bird which I shot in Sierra Leone. This morning we, the mids, were fishing from the poop for some large red fish which we saw swimming about and jumping about but we could not catch any, one fellow got hooked one and then landed it nearly up to where he was, when it broke the line and got away and another one backed off with a bit of somebody else's line. I expect this is the last or nearly last letter that you will get from me for some time because we are going into some out of the way places where the mails don't come. I dined in the wardroom the other night with Mr Pittman, the naval instructor, and a few nights before with the First Lieutenant (in future I shall call him "number one" as we all call him on board) because he is the First Lieutenant or first officer. We are expecting the mail in to take our letters home. Give my best love to dear granny and Nora and Maude, Dico and the babies. We play a lot of whist in the gun room for 3d. a point. I am at present 75 points to windward – or, as you would say, I have won 75 points – and there is only one more day before the end of the month, and we pay up at the end of the month. There is no harm in playing as long as I take care to stop when I am too much to leewards.[15] We never or nearly never play backgammon now. Now once more goodbye, much love and kisses to everyone, please do send as many photos as you like.

HMS *Dido* at anchor off Lagos, October 2, 1879

Just a line to say I am well. It is only two days ago that I wrote my last letter so there cannot be much to say. The mail goes in about one hour. This is the place where there are supposed to be such an immense number of sharks. I have not

---

15 in debt

seen any yet, but then we have only just come in. Perhaps we are going to fish for one soon. It is quite dangerous landing here I believe because you have to cross the bar which shifts and if you get landed on it the boat turns over, being capsized by the surf, and then eaten by sharks which swarm off there in hundreds. And if you don't go in a small boat a steamer comes off to the ship but the said steamer cost £5 to come off so I don't expect many of us will land. After this we are going to the River Bonny, where they say the natives are fighting and stopping the white men trading. The gist of it is I believe that two natives want to make themselves kings. I should be very glad if you would send me some foreign paper and envelopes. We are going to stay here till the outward bound mail comes in. I hope I shall get a lot of mail, a lot of nice letters from you all. Give my best love to granny and aunt. Now I must wind up and kisses to Nora, Maud, Dico and the babies.

HMS *Dido*, Lagos, October 7th 1879

I have just been told to go up to school in the Captain's cabin, where we always do school so I cannot go on writing now but I will go on afterwards!! (1:45 pm) we have had luncheon, but not in the gun room as we usually do because why, oh why, because an enormous sea has come into the port and drenched everything so we had luncheon outside the mess on the table without the legs, which we placed on the chests. The mail from home arrived here at about 4 o'clock this morning so I got your dear letter, Mother, which I enjoyed thoroughly. I am so glad you enjoyed yourself at dear old Rockenham. I am surprised at you going over to Ireland on such a rough night as you did. I hope you were not very sick!!

I like Dr Atkinson very much., better and better every day, he is very nice to me. Last night we were both sitting on a skylight in the dark talking to each other. I was talking to him about Wickford and the Orwell (he is Irish by the way) and fishing with you, Papa, in South Wales and in fact he is very nice to me and the First Lieutenant is also awfully jolly to me. The other day he asked me into the wardroom to have a glass of sherry with him and he showed me the photograph books of his. He knows Lady Grey. Oh, no, I remember, if I have told you of it before, but mind and don't send me any more *Sporting and Dramatic* newspapers, because we take it in in the gun room. You can send me any *Illustrated London News* if you happen to have any, but I don't want you to buy any more for me thanks. Mother says in her letter to me we must soon go on to the Cape, but I don't expect we will go to the Cape for about another three or four months or more probably. This is fortunately the healthy part of the year here being winter and I hope when summer comes on we may go to the Cape out of the way of the fever. I wonder where we will spend Christmas. It will be only the second Christmas I have spent away from you all. The other Christmas I spent away was when you, mother, was ill at home, and Dico and myself spent Christmas someplace near the New Forest with Uncle Thurston[?] or somebody.

I hope the Zulu war is not over because if it is not perhaps we shall go to the Cape sooner. They say that Sir Garnet Wolseley hates the Navy so I don't expect that he would have much fun. I hope, Papa, you will have some trout fishing as you have stayed in Norway after Major Forbes left. I bought a service ditty box the other day, price 2/3, a very useful machine. It is about 1 foot long and 6 inches high and 8 broad, and is empty except a place to hold pens in, and a small place for an ink bottle or something of the sort. All the men have one to keep their curios in. It has also got a place to hold papers in the lid; they are very strong boxes only they have not got good locks. I keep a lot of things in it, besides all the letters I have received since I left England. The one you sent last makes 25, I think altogether, that I have received. I should very much like to see Rockenham now that it is done up again.

I have got all your letters for some time back. I think I only missed about four letters altogether. I am so happy when I get a letter I like it better than anything. I have just put a new nib into my pen and it is very sharp, I think I shall change it soon. I was surprised in mother's letter, she did not say anything about Captain's Wright's death. How funny you should not have heard of it before. We were surprised at not seeing our new Captain's name in the paper. I wonder who he will be. I am in an awful state about the clothes F and D sent me. I have not received them yet. Write and tell me please that they are addressed! I only sent two dozen things on shore here to be washed so it will cost me only 6/- instead of about 15/– which it would have had been if I had sent all my dirty clothes … I am perfectly well, you might like to know, before I go any further. I am glad James came to see you, Mother. I should have thought that he would not have liked coming back to Rockenham after living like that. You must have liked going to Dunmore, Mother. I hope you also got a nice table for dear granny. The girls must have been very glad that you would not let them go on to England because of the castle. I expect Dico and the babies enjoyed themselves at Severn House while you were at Rockenham, he must have had such fun with the dear babies. It will be a great loss to the Aunts and Granny when the Powers have gone. I hope you enjoyed your picnic. I send you some poetry that has been composed by one of the Marines on board the ship about Captain Wright's death and was printed at Sierra Leone. I am so very sorry about poor Flag. I hope he will soon be well again. I began to do a painting of Sierra Leone but it was too hot and I made a mess of it. I hope you won't mind!!! I should like to have seen you driving up to Rockenham on an outside car, I can imagine you laughing at seeing everybody stare at you. I suppose nobody expected you. Have you seen Darling Beppy, you said nothing about her in your letter. And now I think I will tell you about our firing off the 100lb.torpedo and the sharks. (I think I'll continue this letter tomorrow or this evening because I want a cup of tea now so goodbye, all, for the present.)

(8.30 same day) Now I will tell you about the torpedo. We lowered him into the water on the end of the lower boom to about 45 feet from the ship. The torpedo is made of iron, shaped like a tube and painted red, and weighs about 160lb altogether. Well, when we had lowered him into the water we fired and the thing went off and shook the ship terribly – hurt the engines and sent an enormous column of water nearly as high as the topsail yardarm, the spray going higher still and then water came rushing up. I cannot explain it to you but perhaps if you blow a smaller one off in the bath you will see it!! But then we all looked anxiously for fish, especially sharks. Well, hundreds and hundreds of fish came up and some of the officers say they saw one or two sharks amongst them but they went down again. The cutter which was already lowered, rushed amongst the fish picking up all they could see. The fish consisted of only two sorts, catfish, which are not fit to eat and which sting badly, they did sting some Kroomen, and the other kind was a kind of enormous bass which are fit to eat. Well, suddenly I saw them lowering the dinghy so I accordingly jumped into her and we were lowered into the water. I thought we were going to capsize on the way down but we did not and when we were in the water I found Mr Charteris the navigating Lieutenant hanging onto the rope ladder, he had missed his jump into the boat, so we went and got him and pulled away to secure some fish. Well, we picked up about seven bass, the smallest of which weighed over 10lb., after a great deal of bother and danger because the sharks might at any moment have come and snapped at our fingers. The last fish the three boats that were away had had a fight for, because some of the fish sank when you touched them because they were only half stunned. Well, this was one of them, but Mr Charteris hit him with a boat hook, so we secured him and came on board with our spoils.

When all the fish were laid out on the deck numbering in all 34 of these enormous bass, none of which weighed under 10lb. [We had] a machine that weighed up to 32lb, but we could not weigh the biggest, which we imagine must have weighed over 40lb. They were all given out to the ship's company, the wardroom and ourselves, taking care to secure a nice tender one and they were certainly very good. We are supposed to fire off a 100lb torpedo every six months. While we were away a man fell overboard, he reached the gangway and got on board safe but he would most certainly have been eaten by sharks if the torpedo had not gone off just before and it had frightened all the sharks away. This is a dreadful hole. There is no fresh meat or provisions so we are living on salt grub and preserved things. The First Lieutenant thought he would fire off a 2 pounds torpedo in the water to see if we could get any fish, so we fired it off but got no fish. Captain Allen has been onshore for about four days, I don't know when he is going to come on board again. I have just used the last bit of paper which you sent me out, I am now using some paper which Colmore gave me. When we arrived here we found the *Dwarf*, and Colmore came on board. We were all very glad to see him. And now, darling Father and Mother, goodbye, love and kisses to Granny, the aunts, Dico, Nora, Maud and the babies. The ship is getting nicely decorated by degrees and at St Helena we are going to have fine decorations. I send you one of the scales of the big fish we got.

October 9, 1879, Lagos, Sunday

I went on shore yesterday in the steamer, we crossed the bar but it was a very calm day and we got very little sea on board of us, so we went onshore. When we got onshore I went off with Chapell who is acting paymaster, because our other paymaster was invalided, and went off to Mr Porter's, a kind of large merchant, about some grub. After wandering about we found his house in a kind of yard with a wall round it and he was awfully nice. He gave us some lunch and after lunch we laid out outside on sofas and smoked cigars, that is Mr Porter and Chappell did. Then after that we wrote our names in his birthday book and I tried on his jockey's coat and cap, and his hunting coat and cap. Then he went to look for some horses for us because Lagos is the only place on the coast where horses will live, but he only had three and one of them was sick, and then he was going to drive one in his trap and he lent the other one to Chappell, and took me in the trap with him so off we went. We left Chappell after a little (Porter was awfully unhappy about his horse because Chappell could not ride and the horse kept stumbling) so after Porter had done a few things we came back to his place when he sent me off with a black guide to show me about, but I gave him threepence to pocket, which he did. As I was walking along I saw Bruce and Williams, and I went on and I went into their place, which was a kind of empty room on the top of the house. They had just been having some cocoa and biscuits and sardines, so I went below and bought a pot of cocoa for ninepence and two biscuits, twopence, and had some water boiled, then I had some cocoa and biscuits. I drank nearly all the cocoa except one cup, which Williams had. Then we went out and went into the shop where we come humbugged a black man, a schoolmaster, and Bruce bought a bit of discoloured ivory for one shilling and then they went towards the place to go to the steamer, so I went in the direction of Porters house to say goodbye, but I met him driving Chappell down so I got in and we all went down together and went on board the steamer, before doing which I and Bruce went to heave up some lines belonging to some natives to see if there when were any fish on them but the natives came out awfully excited, so we went away. I forgot to tell you that Porter gave me a toy!! A kind of box which you twisted about and saw wonderful figures,[16] and I gave the aforesaid toy to Bruce. Then we crossed over the bar again, shipping only about three seas over our bows but rolling and pitching fearfully and got on board. We were very disappointed at not having any big seas come right over us like they generally do crossing the bar. If you fall overboard near the bar anywhere it is certain death, because it is crowded with sharks Last night the steamer, which was anchored close to us, caught two hammerhead sharks. Now I'm going to luncheon. I will finish afterwards. They are going to bring one of the hammerhead sharks on board this afternoon.

And now I have finished my lunch, which took up four minutes. I had about five spoonfuls of pea soup and a glass of wine, there was potted salmon and four potted lobsters going cheap but I am heartily sick of both these. The mail is going this afternoon and it is now 1215. I did not tell you how long I was onshore: I went at 11 o'clock and came back at 5 o'clock. Mr Porter has a house where the officers often sleep when onshore. Lagos is a much better place than Sierra Leone. The only disadvantage is that there are no baths. It is perfectly level, which Sierra Leone certainly was not. Now, goodbye all. I hope that Granny and the Aunts see my letters because I don't write many letters, because it is stupid writing the same thing all over again. I forgot to tell you that last night we had a whist tournament of eight fellows, each fellow putting in two shillings, and I and another fellow Barry (assistant engineer) won it, so I got six shillings. I am getting on in whist.

HMS *Dido*, at anchor, Off Brass River, one of the mouths of the Niger

[*To Miss H. Morris*] I am so very sorry to hear about poor old Flag. What a pity, but you must get another dog instead of him. Thanks for your nice letter, it was very interesting. I will send you a wing as soon as I can get one for you

---

16 probably a type of kaleidoscope

to have. We have just come from Lagos and are at present at anchor off Brass River which is one of the mouths of the River Niger. We are about 6 miles off the shore, very uninteresting. We are waiting for the mail to take our letters home. After we have given our letters to the mail we are going down to the Bonny River which is 150 miles off, to quiet the natives because they are kicking up a row and fighting. We are going to fire off our rockets and guns et cetera at a target to frighten them, it will be a rare joke. How is Granny and Aunt Jet[?] I hope they are all well and happy. I believe you get all the letters I send home to Mother and Papa to read, because I don't write many to you because you see them. We play a great deal of whist in the gun room, I am very fond of it. We took five cows on board at Lagos, we have killed them all now in three days. We had to throw the meat of one overboard because it was bad. It is awfully hot, 94° [34°C] in the sun at midday. Our First Lieutenant is awfully jolly (Mr Michaelson) he is very nice to me, so is the doctor, Atkinson – he is Irish, they're both awfully jolly to me. Captain St Clair is [also] very nice to me and I'm sorry to say he is ill, and he often has slight touches of fever. That is better than one bad attack. I'm perfectly well, I'm glad to say. I saw a large shark last Sunday. One of the Sub-Lieutenants shot him with a rifle and missed him, and he gave an enormous splash, went down soon again but he soon came up again with his large fin above water and then went down again for good. We fished for him with some pork but could not catch him.

Now goodbye, and remember me to the Potters.

HMS *Dido* just off the mouth of the Niger, going in this evening, October 13, 1879

I have sat down with the intention of writing a letter before but I am afraid that I will have hard work to find something to tell you. We are at present near the mouth of the Niger, where we are going a little way into anchor and wait for the mail to take our letters home. I have just written to Boyle in the *Monarch* in the sweet Mediterranean. After this we are going onto the Bonny where we are going to frighten the natives, who are creating a disturbance, by firing off rockets, guns et cetera at a target, then we will go down the South Coast which is very nice and then off to St Helena and Ascension. On Sunday I saw my first shark and, by Jove, it was enormous. It was cruising about with its enormous fin above water, close to the ship. Lindsay fired at him with a rifle but he missed him, so he gave a tremendous splash and went down but came up soon afterwards, then went down again for good, we fished for him with pork but could not catch him. We caught some catfish on smaller hooks. Catfish have a sharp thing on their back which stings and hurts very much. We have just been doing seamanship, I was sent up to the top gallant masthead to find out something and now I have just come down and am very hot. I'm writing to you and have just made a cup of hot cocoa which I'm going to drink now. By the next outward mail I'm expecting money from you … I cannot think of anything else to say now. If the mail does not go too soon, I will write some more. And now all love, dear ones and Granny, Aunts et cetera.

HMS *Dido* Fernando Po, October 26, 1879, Sunday

I received your very nice letters and enclosed in them the cheque. I am so very much obliged to you …

We heard yesterday that the Commodore is coming up the coast, and then we shall go down to the Cape which will be delicious, that will be in about six weeks we expect, and if we meet him, one of the mids will probably leave the ship to go to the *Boadicea*, the Commodore's ship, and I expect it will be the junior mid. We also discovered last night by the papers that a Captain Domvile, or some such name, was appointed to us and as he is very strict we are very distressed because we expect to always have to wear frock coats on deck and won't be allowed to sleep on the poop on a hot afternoon. Thanks so much for the papers, I like them very much but I don't want any more *Sporting or Dramatic*, because we take them in. I told you that before though.

I caught a shark the other day in this place, it measured 6'6". I was on the poop looking about when I looked down and saw this shark swimming along just close alongside the ship with its young one swimming on the top of it and a lot of pilot fish piloting him about, so I yelled out to some officers who were on the poop who came and looked at him. When it then went forward looking for grub we at once sent down for a shark hook and a lump of pork and lowered it overboard. Well, the shark then came and bit it and we hauled him up and got his head above water when the brute fell off. Well we again lowered the hook just under the water and he came again and bit it. This time we let him have it so when he had swallowed it we hauled him up and it took four men to do it and having two running bowlines over him to prevent him going again, we let him hang over the ships side to exhaust him. Lt. Charteris, our navigating lieutenant, fired two bullets into his head, which nearly finished him so we hauled him on board and then he was measured (6'6") and the blue jackets hauled him forward and opened his belly to see what was in it and the only thing they found was a sheep's hoof and he bit somebody, fingers too. We then had his jaws cut out because his teeth were wanted and one of the clerks got his backbone which smells. I send you home the two sharks teeth which

Dr Atkinson gave me; they make awfully nice pins set in gold, he said. Please keep one of them safe for me because I should like to have it made into a pin when I go home because it would be nice to have a pin made of the tooth of the first shark I saw caught. Mr Michaelson (Number One) you know what Number One means, First Lieutenant, has given me a photo of the *Dido* like the one you have.

I am so glad you, Papa, enjoyed yourself in Norway I wish I could have some of the nice cold water you spoke about down here. I should like to see the fine elk horn you brought back with you. It will look nice over the dining room door or where ever you put it. We are all well on board, one blue jacket has had a bad attack of fever but he is nearly all right now, evidently it is a good thing that fever is not infectious. After we leave here we are going up the Bonny River for about a fortnight. I expect we will get our new Captain there and Captain St Clair (who is well) will leave us there too. I wish you could send me out a few cartridges. Don't send them before you are pretty certain where to send them to.

I am a great shooter and often get hold of a few cartridges to go into the bush or on the shore shooting the land snipe and other birds. You have no idea how wild and hard it is to get near the snipe. The other day along the beach, about 6 miles from the ship, I stalked two of these birds for quite 20 minutes each, lost one of them and only wounded the other. After all the wounded one ran into the bush where I could not follow it. I shot some other land snipe though and one very good pigeon which I gave to Capt St Clair for breakfast as he was not very well. I always go about without shoes and stockings onshore when we go up to the beach because there is a river up there where you get most birds and you have to wade up and across it so it is comes rather hard on your feet running over the hard stones and in danger of being pinched by crabs, but I don't mind it, it does not hurt my feet like it does the other fellows and you would think I was mad if you saw me racing along the beach with no shoes on.

The other day the mids went up on an expedition of this sort and went up the river shooting. When we came down again the boat was high and dry, we did our best to get it off but could not as the tide would not be in for four hours so I passed away the time and took my little gun (which I am very fond of) with me and some cartridges, and away I went up the beach after land snipe. Having been away for two and half hours I came back with two cartridges and one snipe and sat down and rested. Then we thought we would have some prize shooting so there were five of us, so we kept the small target, little more than a foot square and put it up 50 paces away on the ground and

we were to shoot at it each putting in one shilling to the sweepstakes, which
was a total of five shillings. Well Chapell, the Clerk, shot first. He put in five
shots, Williams 13 shots, Bruce eight, Nicholson six and Faussett 25 about,
so Mr Godfrey-Faussett carried off the prize with flying colours. Mind you,
none of them would use my gun – oh dear no, it was not so good as the other
double-barrelled ones – but I have great faith in my little gun and if I had been
offered to shoot with the other ones which cost about £25 I should not have
accepted the offer. My little gun is a good gun, it has done little for me yet but
has carried straight as a rule. Yesterday I went on shore with five cartridges
and shot some pretty birds. You might not think it but I am quite a good shot,
with my own eyes!!! The only thing I am afraid of is that it will not be safe to
fire bullets out of it, which I will want to do when we get to big game down the
coast. You may laugh at this but I mean it!! It I am glad you had a nice passage
from Ireland, not like the one you went over in. I'm very sorry about poor Mr
Batho. I hope he will get all right again. There have been two fishing days. On
the first one I went with we did not catch many fish. We had four hauls and
we were in the water the whole time. I had a pair of flannel drawers on and
a jersey, and there we were diving about and swimming about, in danger the
whole time of being eaten by sharks, and when they were hauling in the fish
the little sprats and sardines were jumping about in the air over the net and I
went out then to them and was simply bit all over the face with these fish. I
held up my cap and caught two or three of them. Then we came on board all
dripping wet. Yesterday forenoon we went away in the gig and we bathed in a
small bay, not in the least afraid of the sharks but I don't expect they come in
close. And now I must say goodbye to all … I may be able to add a line before
we send our letters

HMS *Dido* October 28, 1879, Just outside the Bonny River

In two more days I shall be 16 years old, my first birthday at sea spent on the
West Coast of Africa, a long way from where all my other birthdays have been
spent!! Is it not?

We have just stopped to pick up an empty canoe which we saw drifting out
at sea. We left Fernando Po yesterday at 1 o'clock and are now just outside the
Bonny waiting for the mail to take our letters home and then we are going up
to the Niger to meet the *Pioneer* because our Sub, Lindsay, went on board that
ship in place of Harwell who was seedy, Harwell coming on board us because
the *Pioneer* was going up the Niger to fight or have some row, and he has not
been well enough. So now that they have been up we are going to get Lindsay
back again … I was very sorry to leave Fernando Po, it was such a nice place,

one of the prettiest places in the world with its enormous high mountains, 10,000 feet high, and the beautiful trees and little bays and magnificent sunsets and then you could see the magnificent Cameroon mountains, 14,000 feet high and more than 40 miles away from us. There was a Spanish man of war in Fernando Po when we were there. It was smaller than us and very dirty and the yards were not squared properly. There is one of the mids with the fever very slightly. I and one other are the only mids who have not as yet been seedy, except for seasickness of course … We expect to get to St Helena in about a month's time. I shall be very glad. I should like to spend Christmas rather at St Helena or the Cape, the Cape best of course. Thanks very much for the newspaper cutting about the Princes. Did you see those pictures in the *Graphic* about the Bacchante? Halve all the pictures and you will be nearer the mark. They are all tremendously exaggerated. I expect we will have to go to seamanship instruction now. I expect we are going to get our letters from England at this place, I hope we do. I am really stumped for something to say so goodbye. Love to all in England and Ireland

HMS *Dido* off the Nun Entrance to the Niger River, November 3, 1879

I have got very bad news to tell you. Jolly old Colmore is going to be invalided home, he has had a bad attack of fever and he is going home this afternoon. You know he went to the *Dwarf* for a short time and he came back the other day bringing with him the new Captain. Well, poor Colmore is going home and we are awfully sorry, especially myself. I suppose we will have another Sub Lt sent out in his place. I gave him a nice little matchbox, I had one with an anchor of it and he was very pleased with it. I'm also sending home two things by him, my dressing case and my letter writing case because I'm too fond of them both to let them remain in the mess any more getting kicked about and spoiled, so I send them home by Colmore, they're going to his outfitters who is to pack them up and send them home. I know you would rather have them at home than out here with me, getting spoiled, because they're only an anxiety to me. The address of his outfitters is Salt, Grieve and Company, High Street, Portsmouth.

Mr Charteris, our navigating Lt, is also going home for the same reason, and also two or three men. Bruce (mid) who had the fever when I last wrote is better now, but not off the sick list. I have not been seedy yet I'm thankful to say.

They say that they are going to take this ship off the station at once, so that

we will go to Australia or the Pacific. I have put one or two little things into
the dressing case for you all. The card case and cigarette case I got at Madeira,
and the shell I picked up with some other good ones at Fernando Po on the
beach when I was stalking birds with my gun, and no shoes or stockings on. It
was the prettiest one I picked up. I have not got a monkey, and I won't bring
one home if I do get one, as you don't like it. I will bring my grass hammock
home with me if I have it. I hope uncle Ernest is better by this time, please
give them all my love. How nice about dear little May B. and her little prayer.
I cannot say I had a very jolly birthday for some things – we got three hours
cutlass and rifle drill for being up late for one morning drill and the first
lieutenant afterwards let me have a large salt water bath on quarterdeck. It is
the rule to stand Champagne and bitter booze on your birthday, and I was not
going to be behindhand so I stood some and it amounted to 18/3d for 3 pints of
champagne and a bottle of sherry, and they presented me with a plum pudding
and cake which was put down to the mess and then I gave Martin some beer.
All the fellows do much the same, some more and some less, so that I'm sure
you won't mind it. I think I would like the *Illustrated News* or *Funny Folk*
instead of *Sporting and Drama Review*, because we take it on board. And
now I'm afraid I know not what more to say. I wrote a nice long letter to uncle
Robert at Oxford and sent him a photo of the *Dido* which Mr Michaelson had
given me. And now goodbye. Love and kisses. Colmore is going to post this in
England for me.

HMS *Dido*, at Anchor off Fairway Buoy of the mouth of the Bonny, November 8, 1879

Since I last wrote to you the *Pioneer* has come back and Lindsay has come
on board again. I hope you got my last letter, the one which Colmore posted
in England. Well, they had some fighting up the Niger. A hundred white and
black men from two towns were fighting against 10,000 natives all the time.
You will probably see about it in the papers. Nobody on our side was killed,
but some few of our black men were wounded and one is expected to die, but
a heap were killed on the natives' side – Lindsay brought a lot of poisoned
arrows, a bow and a dagger and a beautiful long spear and a fetish. I think that
was about all. The knife is an iron thing with an iron loop in the top into which
you fit your hand so that you could fire the bow and arrow and then if your
opponent came too near you, you could then use the knife but the natives had
rifles. They had quite an adventure, and if the blacks had only been wise they
could have surrounded the white men and massacred the whole lot, so they
came down talking all about their adventures – Lindsay has now got the acting

lieutenancy because Mr Ogle has taken on navigating duties.

I made Colmore promise to write to me and send me his photographs before he went. Dear old Captain St. Clair went away the other day to take passage to his own ship, the *Dwarf*, on the *Pioneer*. I waited at the gangway to say goodbye to him, everybody in the ship liked him. All the mids have got a plan of the lower deck of the ship to do for the First Lieutenant, and he is going to give a prize for the best. Mine is a very fair one as yet, but I don't expect to get the prize. We have just had the thermometers down here for ¼ of an hour and it rose to 90° [32°C]. We are all working in our jerseys and perspiring like rain. This is the third time we have been anchored off the Bonny, and each time about 16 miles off the land. Please send me some foreign paper and envelopes as soon as you can and please remind Fraser that he has not sent me the two No.3 watch bills that I wrote to him for on August 4, 1879. I expect the next mail will be with you just on Christmas Day. I must manage to write by that mail and now there is really no more news to tell you. Love to all.

HMS *Dido* off the Bonny, November 11, 1879

I will just add a line, the mail goes this afternoon and we are going up Bonny for the first time. It is a very dangerous navigation so we may probably go aground now by all best love to everyone.

HMS *Dido* in Bonny River, November 15, 1879

There is lots of news but I don't know where to begin!!! Because on here a few days ago, navigation is rather difficult, especially as we have not a proper navigating lieutenant, only our Gunnery Lieutenant who has taken up navigating duties. Well, we came in without getting aground. I went into the mizzen top to have a look round, and while I was up there I saw amongst other things what I thought was a fish about 9 feet long going along on the top of the water, dipping down now and then going on again altogether for about 10 yards when I came down again I told Dr Atkinson (he is awfully jolly to me) and he said that he thought it must have been a snake of some kind to see exactly what it was. It is rather pretty but the town Bonny is very unhealthy being in the middle of the mangrove swamp, and all the white people agents et cetera live in large hulks at anchor in the river. The King of Bonny ("King George Pepper") is away at present, and the biggest swell here, Oko Jumbo, has a large pretentious looking house near the landing place. I have not been on shore yet, I don't expect I will be allowed to go on shore because it is so unhealthy Oko Jumbo has about 50 sons and daughters. Eight of his sons have been to England for education, and the eldest one John Jumbo is very nice. Coming in the other day we passed about 30 small canoes fishing. There are lots of fish but these children seldom bring them to the ship to sell until after they are stale. Now I think I must have finished with the descriptions of the place so good night all.

Scene I. Gun room, four midshipmen with ditty boxes writing letters home. The thermometer about 90° [32°C], mids all in their shirts, one is writing at the end of the table saying as follows – I am now about to go on with this long epistle. Since I last wrote to you wonderful things have taken place, and I believe the details of it described in the newspapers are also pictured in the *Graphic*. The 'great', it being translated into another language, means Palaver.[17] Well you must be getting rather sick of all that nonsense. I will proceed, but before I proceed, as I believe that this letter will reach home on or about Christmas Day I wish you all "a very Merry Christmas and happy New Year and May you all have many of them". And now I proceed. There has been a row for some time up river between the New Calabar Kings and Chiefs, and Bonny, the Opobo and Will Braid, a very powerful chief. The cause of it all is this Will Braid, who is a chief of Calabar, and as he was very powerful and very rich the Calabar Ministers wanted to put him down but two of them, John Bull and Horsefoot [?] especially wanted to put him down, so they inflicted very heavy fines on Will Braid and Yellow, another great chief. So these two chiefs took all their possessions and ran away and took up a very strong position on the banks of the River Bonny and stopped all trading, so that is what the palaver is about because the trading is stopped. The Bonnarians are siding with Will Braid, and the Opoborians are siding with the Calabars, so the Palaver took place yesterday, or at least the beginning of it, the rest is going on today. We have taken all the guns off except one on the Quarterdeck, and put a large table there and about 100 chairs for the Chiefs to sit upon. While our Captain, the Consul and Will Braid, Oko Jumbo (King Bonnie) Prince Jaja son of King Jaja of Opobo and King of New Calabar, and also the Ministers viz. Corking, Prime Minister of Opobo – Addo Alison, chief of Bonny and father of 20 sons, (not counting daughters), Yellow Chief with Will Braid and the chief of the Bonny all sat round the table. First there were about 200 chiefs and kings and their attenders on board, and in the canoes about 750 slaves altogether. I have made you a little sketch of all the canoes hanging on stern [not included in this transcription]. First of all the Captain made a speech and

---

17 formal negotiations/talks

informed them that any tribe which did not agree to the terms decided on by the Consul and the Captain would be heavily fined and would be considered as enemies of the Queen. Then the Consul gave another speech much the same as the Captain's, and then the different chiefs and kings told their complaints. Will Braid's speech was translated by a man, and it said that one of the men was captured by the Calabar men, they cut his tongue out and made a Ju-ju god out of it and ate his body, and then the other people spoke and so on. Then they broke up, and each country went to a different part of the ship to try to come to an arrangement, but I don't believe they have arrived at one yet. Then they broke up altogether and went away at sunset in their canoes beating tom-toms and playing wooden drums. And now they are at work today and I doubt they are any nearer signing the agreement than they were yesterday. The officers have to wear their cocked hats and epaulettes and tail coats.

Now I'll give you an account of the different important chiefs. They nearly all wear long shirts and beautiful ivory bracelets and magnificent coral beads. Each of the coral beads is worth about £5, and they all wear beautiful caps, smoking caps. I have got one of the ivory bracelets, I gave a man nine shillings for one! He was not a chief, but it is a very good one but not as good as some. I have also got two very funny straw caps with a grass castle on the top of them. I gave sixpence for two, the natives here wear them – nearly all the boys under 18 go about naked. There is a Ju-ju house onshore full of the skulls of their enemies and people they have sacrificed. But I am wandering away from my description of the Kings. Will Braid is a funny little man, very fat, he wears a long black wig. Most of the chiefs are fine big men. The King of Calabar is a very funny little old man and I have made a great friend of one of his ministers, John Bull, the man who used to run down Will Braid. I gave him two brass buttons, and he is going to wear them round as a Ju-ju. They shake hands in a very funny way – I am high up in the art of how they shake each other's hands. We are going to have some theatricals soon, I believe, in which I am cast. And now the mail is going so goodbye, I will finish in my next letter.

HMS *Dido* Bonny River
November 21, 1879

I am afraid that my last letter was not much of a one, it was written in a great hurry. This one may perhaps reach you about New Year's Day so I wish you all in Ireland and England 'A happy new year, and many of them'. The Palaver is now over, (on the evening of the day that I sent my last letter) it was finished. The Chiefs had all signed or rather made their mark, and had rose up to go away when one of them said they had better have another palaver on the next day about some markets, so it was arranged that they should be on board again by 11 o'clock next day, and it was fortunate that they did arrange to have a palaver because when these two tribes, Bonny's and Calabar's set up to go away, there was a new war declared between them about their markets, but of course it was stopped when they decided upon having the new palaver. Well, the Palaver came off and it was arranged to take one of the Calabar's markets away from the Calabar and give it to the Bonny men. It was about one hour before the Calabars could be induced to sign the treaty, but the Skipper frightened them into it by telling them that if they did not sign it they would be enemies of the Queen and all their trade will be stopped, so they at last signed and went away contented.

I think I told you something about the canoes in my last letter, they have on average 30 natives in each, one to steer with one big paddle two to beat tom-toms, one to beat the drum and the remainder to pull or rather to paddle. The Chiefs or Kings have a place in the middle to sit on, and in the canoe there is a long chest full of rifles and other chests with pistols and swords in them; men and boys that paddle boats are all slaves, and are paid from £5 to £15 for each of them. There was one old chief who was on board was the father of 90 sons, to say nothing of daughters!!! I asked Will Braid down into the gun room on Thursday. We gave him some lunch and a glass of rum. He is a very nice old man but smells. Oh dear! He took a biscuit out of the dish and nibbled it then put it back again so we had to throw it overboard. He is going to send his son Obadiah, a nice little fellow, to England to be educated, so we had the aforesaid to luncheon on Thursday, and the other night he came on board to see some of our theatricals. He was very cold so I wrapped him up in my rug which he liked very much, and when he went away we gave him an empty ginger beer bottle and one or two other little things. The consul has written a long account of the Palaver to the *Liverpool Mercury* and also the *Daily Telegraph* so I advise you to get these papers if you want a good account of it all, and Mr Pittman (the Chaplain) and Chappell, the clerk, are making two or three sketches of the proceedings which they are thinking of sending to the *Graphic* or *Illustrated Evening News*. One sketch will be the same kind of little one that I sent you.

We are getting up some kind of theatricals in which I'm going to act, very much against my will, the piece in '*Ici on parle français*', and I have to take Angelina's part. I did my very best to get out of it but it was no good, I am hoping that the whole affair will get knocked on the head. I have not seen anything of the clothes which F and D sent me but I'm keeping a good look out for them: they cannot possibly be ready but I wish you would write to F and D about the watch bills number 3, which I wrote to him on August 4th and told him to send at once. I have not seen anything of them. We are going out of this place tomorrow I believe, and then we wait outside for the mail from home then we are going on to Ambas Bay, a very nice healthy place where we will all be able to go onshore and do lots of shooting. I went out shooting here in a boat the other day with two other guns, but we only got one large white heron and two sand snipe, all shot on the wing except one snipe, and then we came on board. We had to take a lot (of awful) doses of quinine which all but turned me up.

I forgot to say that while we were away we saw whole flocks of beautiful parrots fly across overhead just out of reach of our guns. I wish I knew where we are going to spend Christmas. I was in hopes that it would be at the Cape but that is almost impossible now. We might possibly spend it at St Helena. I have found three cards in my box which I send home. I have not sent them to anybody in particular because three cards cannot be divided amongst so many. I have got a nice ivory bracelet which I got off a native for ninepence. I cannot send it home. I have also got two dunces caps made out of straw that I gave sixpence for. The natives wear them onshore. I have not written to granny because you can send this letter all round the family I would only tell her exactly the same things.

All Love to all

HMS *Dido* Ambas Bay, November 27, 1879

I got a lot of letters last mail, one from you, mother, dated October 9, one from Norah, cousins Alfred and Cecil, and Granny, they were all nice and long. Just before we came out of the Bonny a biggish steamer signalled to us that her crew of blacks had risen up in mutiny so we sent an officer and after him we sent six Marines and a sergeant who brought back four of the blacks, the ringleader in handcuffs and after standing on the quarter deck for about one hour, our Captain sent them on board again with the Marines where the ringleader got three dozen instead of the four dozen and the other three 2 dozen across the back with a stick, and then they were sent onshore, the clothes having been taken from them. A filter (the same size as the one at home) has just fallen down on the top of the fellow's head and he is slanging it roundly now. The rolling of the ship brought it down and the filter is smashed – you say in your letter to me to give Captain St Clair your kind regards. I'm sorry to say I cannot because he has gone away back to the *Dwarf*.

When we left Bonny we went on to Fernando Po where we saw the Spanish gunboat which we had seen there before and which stays in place six months out of the year. She had got all her yards down and was evidently repairing so we sent our washing onshore intending to call for it after we leave this place, then we came on here into this lovely Ambas Bay. This is a most beautiful place. I will just try and give you an idea of our position. There are a lot of small islands, one of them a long high rock shaped like a pillar, one of them called Pirate Island, where pirates were supposed to have lived in the days of yore. There's also the wonderful Cameroon mountain, 13,000 feet high. Nothing but trees up to the very top, almost all round everywhere there are nothing but trees on high hills or mountains. The Cameroon mountains and all the surrounding mountains are almost always shut up in clouds here and there, but we have once or twice been able to see the whole thing clear, but there is no use trying to tell you how wonderful it is, but one island that I want to tell you about, this being the only place I have yet been to see. I and two or three other gunroom fellows, the Doctor, Chaplain and Captain went in the steam cutter and steamed in this round the island. We saw what the Captain said was a white headed eagle also a cockatoo. At last we came to a place where the waves did not beat so fiercely on the rocks, so we got into the dinghy and landed and then commenced a tedious climb up along almost perpendicular and narrow paths with overhanging plants in some places so thick that it was almost dark, and at last we reached the top, puffing and blowing.

On the top was a village consisting of six huts in a row. When we went into the village all the women ran into the huts, they only have a cloth around their waists and the men the same. So we went and shook hands with all the men, and one little boy who termed himself King William's son acted as interpreter, so we talked a great deal and one of our fellows got up a tree and threw some coconuts down, the juice of which we drank. The women then began to feel bold and then came out and we talked to them. The houses are merely huts made of leaves thatched together in a way and each one had one big room about 12' × 8' and also a small room. The ground is just the earth. They have very funny chairs about half a foot high which you just fit into. Their livestock consists of a lot of what looked like goats more than sheep, but they are called sheep, and we saw one large one with a long mane all round his neck and chased them about the place for something to do. But after we had looked at that village we went to the other one which was close and consisted of three houses on each side of a path. It was much like the same as the other one, only the women were more bashful so the skipper gave King William's son a shilling and we came down again which was much harder than getting up. When we got to the bottom the Captain said we would go off in the canoe, the one we picked up some time back, so one of the Kroomen was in the canoe and the other in the water so the skipper stepped in. Just as he did so a wave came and shoved it forwards so the skipper got overbalanced and both men hung onto him, so the consequence was that the canoe capsized and the three of them got a ducking while we roared at them onshore. The Captain did not mind a bit and began laughing heartily at it so then we got on board the steam cutter safely and came on board!!!

And now I think I've told you all the news but perhaps you would like to know what we are doing in here. Well, we are refitting ship, we have sent down our top gallant masts and top sail yards and are setting up lower rigging et cetera. The ship is in an awful mess but we expect to get out back to Fernando Po in about a week [and] we'll then have been here 10 days. I intend to go onshore the first opportunity but I have no one to go with. I wish you would tell Fraser and Davies please to send me a coat and trousers made of that blue flannel stuff as mine are almost worn out and I wear them night and day because my jacket is not fit to wear …

HMS *Dido*, Fernando Po, December 4, 1879

That letter which is enclosed with this one is the same envelope I wrote about seven days ago and ought to have gone then but there was no steamer to take it. So now I'm going to continue to tell you the remainder of the news only you must read the other one first (they have just passed the word that the mail bag closes in half an hour).

After I wrote you the last letter we had two days of swimming. We started at 4:15 pm on the first day and got back about 7:30 pm but the second day we did not get back until 10 o'clock, It was awful fun, the first day was not much fun we did not get many fish either but the second day was rare fun. We sent the dinghy out and we all followed in the pinnace. The First Lieutenant and two or three of the other officers and all of us mids except one sick one came. I wore a very small pair of flannel trousers, a flannel shirt, coat and a pair of old shoes without socks. When we got to the place, about 2 miles from the ship, we anchored the pinnace and jumped out up to our waists in water having just taken my shoes off and then we lit two large fires onshore and began fishing. We had about a dozen hauls altogether and we got a lot of fish. By this time it was dark so we cooked our fish and sardines (preserved) and had some very hot cocoa and had a nice supper, then I stripped and took off all my clothes and put on a pair of bathing drawers and went and had the most delicious bathe I had ever had, regardless of sharks or anything else. The phosphorus which you made swimming through the water! There were enormous breakers which you could just see in the dark coming along and then you would try and keep your head above the breakers which was rather difficult – in fact it was the most delicious bathe. Then I came in, warmed myself by the fire and put on my trousers and shirt, then we all sat around the fire, about 50 blue jackets and nine officers, the men sang songs and two of the officers. The first lieutenant was one of those who sang a song, and then we got on board the pinnace, a marine carried me on his head because I did not want to get wet again, with some more songs we got on board, had some grub, turned in and I have not got the fever yet! We left Ambas Bay on Thursday and now we are here again for the third time in Fernando Po, and I believe we are going to have another swimming day here. When I got in here we found your letters waiting for us addressed to St Helena (I'm glad to say they did not go there) and we are expecting a mail with some more letters shortly. Then we are going from here probably to San Paul de Loanda and then across to St Helena and Ascension.

Now I will answer your letters. I got nice long ones from Mother, Father and Maud. It will be very nice if I meet Captain Parr when we go to the Cape of Good Hope. I wish we could say, like you say, "It is so cold here." I do so wish you, Papa, would have a photo taken to send me one. My photo book is getting nicely filled up by degrees and it is being nicely kept in the first lieutenant's cabin. Thank you mama very much for the very nice photo of the Queen which you sent me. Has Hilda's poor tooth grown yet? What fun all the festival must have been. Corders shop must be a very big one certainly, from all accounts. Clifton will be quite changed when I get back. You sent me a *Whitehall Review* some time ago, and I looked in the acrostic in the end saw a word written out by Papa and it reminded me very much of the time when you two and I sat in front of the fire in the drawing trying to guess them!! I did not see Hilda's name amongst the correct ones though. I should like to see the new clock, how nice they must both look on the landing. I hope poor Kate and her sisters are well – remember me to Kate and tell her I won't abuse her just yet for not putting water in my jug!!! I have not got the large photo of Dico yet. How soon are you going to have one taken of you, mother in a Cap etcetera … I hope poor Mr Bathe is better now. I will try, Papa, and get butterflies and ferns and flowers small, and squash them in my chest and then I might send some home.

Yesterday we began to coal ship and one of the lighters sank just under our bow full of coal, so we sent divers down after it and one man stayed down a long time and nearly died last night, he was insensible for a long time and the doctor gave him up and today some more went down. I was sent away in the cutter with them for one and a half hours. The diver goes down and hooks a lot

of these bags of coal onto a line and then they are hauled on board. Towards
the end of the time we were just going to haul the man up when he came up in
a rather funny way. We suddenly saw him come up to the top of the water tail
first all blown out with air, tumbling about we thought he was blown up and
dead, but we hauled him on board he said he only came up because he thought
it was the quickest way !!! it was a very foolish thing to do because he might
have been killed if he had fouled one of the lines. And now I think I must stop
because there is nought more to say. With love and kisses to all the Irish ones
and yourselves …

HMS *Dido*, Fernando Po, December 17, 1879

Just a line to say I am quite well. You won't get any more mails for some time.
We are going down to San Paul de Loanda, where I don't believe we will
be able to write much. The mail is just going, it came in this morning and I
got no letters. I was very disappointed but suppose that they have gone to St
Helena. There is not much news, and if there was I would not be able to tell
you because there is no time. I went aboard the other mail yesterday on duty
and had a glass of sherry and a chat. We have finished coaling and the sweat is
rolling off my face and hands. Frightfully hot. I don't know for certain when
we leave here. I dined with the captain, First Lt and Dr and Spanish Governor
last night. It was great fun. I'm writing this on the chest, very uncomfortable. I
am going onshore this afternoon. to stretch my legs as I have not been onshore
for ages and going to buy some things. Now goodbye, love to all. Excuse such
a short epistle.

HMS *Dido*, Fernando Po, December 29, 1879

We are just leaving Fernando Po for San Paul de Loanda. You will not hear
from me again for a very long time, we shall be at sea for weeks. Mail just
going and I have had no time to write, we are in the middle of our half yearly
exams. I shall be nowhere I expect. Mailbag closed.

HMS *Dido*, San Paul De Loando, December 30, 1879

I have not written to you for ages because there was no mail to take the letters,
but we expect a mail soon so I shall begin my epistle. I last wrote to you from
Fernando Po. Well, we left that place and proceeded to Kabuda Bay. It is much
the same as all other places on the coast but it is more hilly. We anchored off
the village, about 2 miles from the shore. It is the only place where there are

supposed to be no sharks, but there certainly are, because the last time Dr Atkinson was here he saw the dinghy capsized and an engineer eaten by a shark; anyhow we used to bathe overboard in the studding sail. I think myself an awful swell because I can dive off the netting of the ship and then swim into the studding sail[18] (you know what the netting is, on top of the bulwarks where they stow the hammocks up).

18 an extra sail, set in light airs

6: The Letters, 1880

January 4, 1880

On the way from Fernando Po to Kabuda Bay we crossed the line, as you
may imagine. Well, we went the through the usual old serious ceremony. On
Saturday we were supposed to cross the line, so on Friday night old Neptune
hailed the ship and was answered by the Officer of the Watch, and the end
of it was that he came on board with the barbers and all the other people. He
came aft onto the poop and spoke to the Captain and to me and to one or two
other mids. He was dressed in top boots and had a lot of oakum for hair. Then
he went down onto the quarterdeck and mounted his carriage (a gun carriage)
and was taken to the gangway when he went away. They have a band of
lighted tar overboard which floated astern and looked like his chariot, And
then, by George, did not you get wet. All the hoses and pumps being rigged,
the blue jackets played the waters over everybody and everything, and then
the proceeding was wound up for the night. I forgot to tell you that he told the
Captain that he will come on board at 1.30 the following day, Saturday, to be
introduced to and to shave all those who had not crossed the line or been into
his domain. The next day at 1:30 pm, punctual to his appointment, he came
on board. There was a studding sail rigged forward, just under the forecastle
which was being constantly filled by a steam hose. On the break of the
forecastle just over the studding sail and about 10 feet above it was placed a
stool. In front of the stool stood Neptune, and around him were his barber and
a lot of other swells, while in the bath were the bears whose duty was to duck
you and push you through to the end of the bath where you are chucked out.

They were about eight bears in all. Well, the procedure was as follows.
We were all down below here (the mids) and two policemen, big men with
bright red painted faces, came and collared you, and you walked up the
ladder between these two men. At the top of the ladder was a hose which they
instantly played on you and wet you through, but that did not much matter as
you only had a jersey and trousers on. Then they led you forward up onto the
forecastle (you were in the utmost danger all the time of breaking your toe
against some obstruction). When you were seated on the stool you were given
your character. If you are not liked they gave you very good as a character but
if you were liked they gave you a very bad character. Then I was asked my
name and several other things but of course I would not open my mouth to

answer so therefore they could not shove any shaving water down my throat (the shaving mixture was made of oatmeal, pease pudding and some other muck) but they rubbed it all over my face, then they took a razor and shaved it all off and then they toppled you backwards into the sail. You were caught by the bears who passed you along, ducking you very much if they did not like you, but I did not get much ducked, then you were kicked out of the sail you then watched everybody else being ducked. None of the officers got it hot, and after us the men had to go through it, they were not blindfolded because it would have taken too long. The Marines were the only ones who did not go through it, there was not time for them. Lindsay happened to be on the sick list at the time or else I suspect he would have got ducked pretty well. There were two kinds of razors, number one and number two. Number two razor was the worst one, it was like a saw and if you were troublesome you got it. Number one was a plain one and did not hurt you much. There was also a smelling bottle which was applied to your nose if you looked at all faint. It had a lot of pins et cetera so to prick your nose and so you may be sure I took good care not to look faint so I did not get the smelling bottle.

Well, I soon went through it all right but I immediately had to go and dress then, because it was my afternoon watch. I had to be keeping watch on the poop while everybody else was enjoying themselves forward on the forecastle. The Master at arms and the writer went and hid themselves in the bread room and locked themselves in, but the policeman were determined not to lose ducking them, so after a lot of hunting about the policeman found out that they were in the bread room so somehow or other after an hour humbugging outside they got the Master at arms to open the door, when they hauled the writer out and ducked him and some time afterwards they gave the Master at arms a real good ducking but there were no real more duckings because the First Lieutenant was on the forecastle. The whole affair ended at 3:30 pm.

And now I'm blowed if I know what to tell you. I think that the first place we went into after crossing the line was Kabuda Bay – it is just the same as all the other bays, not nearly so beautiful as Akuba Bay of course, in fact it is not beautiful at all, nor yet pretty. It is such a long time ago that I don't remember what we did hardly but we used to bathe overboard in the studding sail.

But there is one thing that I must give you an account of while we were there – we went out for a day's fishing. The First Lieutenant and all the gunroom officers came, but we did not take many blue jackets. We took Kroomen instead. When we got onshore we immediately had some lunch and a glass of beer and some potted tongue, on a table cloth on the sand, so all our beer and stuff got full of sand. After I had had some lunch I got my gun and half a dozen cartridges, and with Miall (Assistant Clerk) I went off to see what I could shoot. We went through a swamp but saw nothing but pretty birds which I do not think worth a cartridge, till we came to the end of the swamp. When, up in a tree, Miall pointed out to me what he thought was a monkey so I got where I could see it distinctly and I thought it could be a big cat or monkey or some such animal, but I determined to shoot it, but as the gun was only loaded with shot it did not kill him but wounded him badly so he fell off the bough and hung on by his arms screeching so I loaded again and fired, this time bringing him down plump and dead onto the ground. I did not like to touch him at first for fear he should not be dead and he might bite because he had his eyes open but at last I picked him up and examined him, and he looked exactly like a bear only of course much smaller. If you can imagine a very tiny bear you will know what this thing really was. So I brought him back to the camp where everybody examined him and I gave him in charge of a Krooman who I told to skin it, and now I have sent the skin to you by this mail nicely sewn up by one of the bosuns mates in a piece of canvas and if it does not smell too much I would like you to keep it for me please. Well to continue with my story after I had exhibited my skin I went for a cruise in the canoe, and as I went a long way I found it very hard to get back again as the wind was blowing off the land, then I had a good bathe in spite of the sharks and then I went and helped to haul in the net. We caught very fair fish and amongst others some small sharks about 2 feet long, but I don't believe they grow any size close to the shore. At 7.30 about we had dinner in the dark except what light a huge bonfire of dry sticks gave. But, bother it, I forgot to tell you that before it got dark I went off with my gun on my shoulder and five cartridges in my pocket and no shoes on my feet in search of birds et cetera. I could not go into the jungle because I had no boots on, or else I would have chased a beautiful bird with a long tail. I saw a large cotton tree with no leaves on, only large birds or cotton hanging about all over the twigs and branches. I managed to get one branch which I found on the ground and I intended to send it to you but I cannot find it now. Then I went on and stalked a lot of sand snipe and shot five of them. I missed some and came back with my pocket full of birds feathers and blood. Then after supper we got on board the pinnace and went on board singing songs and arrived on board at 9.30 about.

Then when we left there we came and anchored in the mouth of the River Congo where we spent Christmas (instead of at home) you may like to know that there are no houses, or huts rather, at the mouth of this place. It is utterly uninhabited and nobody went ashore. On Christmas Eve we had a good dinner in the gun room if I remember right, [and] a singsong afterwards. Then on

Christmas Day, well it is a long account to give you and especially difficult
because I have nearly forgotten all about it but I will do my best to give you
a good account of how I spent my first Christmas really away from home and
at sea. About 11 o'clock the Captain and all the officers went round the lower
deck to see all the men's messes. The messes were awfully nicely decorated
and the tables were spread with ducks, chicken and cakes, plum puddings and
biscuits, and at the beginning of each mess there was a blue jacket standing
with two plates of plum pudding and cake in his hand of which you had to take
a little piece to taste. So then I got to the end I found my hand crammed full of
bits of plum pudding cake and biscuits and nuts all mixed up with a little pear,
which the heat had caused to make soft. Nothing much happened till about 2
pm when a petty officer came asked Nicholson (mid) and myself to go up and
have something to eat. Of course we had to go, so they stuffed us with cake
and plum pudding et cetera et cetera and made me drink brandy and water,
which I did not like much but it was great fun altogether. Some of the petty
officers were awfully merry! After we had been there for about seven or eight
minutes the other fellows came up and had something. Then we went back
to the gun room and had sherry and cake, and then I had to keep the 4–6 pm
watch during which four of the "theatrical party" of blue jackets came aft on
the quarterdeck, dressed up, and sang songs which were very amusing, and it
actually made the Captain smile (he did not laugh) but then we went to have
dinner in the gun room (about 6.30). The menu was much the same as the one
which I sent you of New Year's Day, only rather better. Champagne and other
wines flew round with alarming velocity (I am very fond of champagne!!)
After putting the lights out and burning the plum pudding almost to a cinder
we had dessert and sang songs – you might not believe it but I sang a song
and did not get out of time or croak either, "Hearts of Oak" was the name
of it. Then all the blue jackets came round to the mess and wanted to carry
Nicholson round, so they carried him round the lower deck singing 'He's a
jolly good fellow', and then they came and carried me around, and then they
carried everybody around singing the same song, and when they got forward
they stopped and you got down and the petty officers spoke to you, then you
are carried back again, then they did this to all the wardroom officers. The
First Lieutenant they carried round twice. Then we were all invited into the
wardroom where we drank hot punch and sang songs I sang "Ring the bell,
Watchman" and we were all very merry until about 11 o'clock and we all went
to turn in so it certainly was a very Merry Christmas. I enjoyed myself very
well after about 6 pm. I did not enjoy myself until then because I was thinking
of home and what you were all doing.

While having told you all about Christmas day there is nothing to tell you

of until we got down to St Paul do Loando – but I forgot to tell you, after
Christmas Day we went up the Congo a little way to a small village in Banana
Creek to coal ship. It was a very dirty day and the coal was perfectly dry, so
the dirt flew about and by the time my watch was over I was perfectly black
and my eyes full of dust. But I managed after a large expenditure of soap and
water to get it out, and now I will go down to where we were on Sunday just
before we got into St Paul do Loando, where an enormous shoal of porpoises
swum towards us. There must have been thousands of them, they leapt high
out of the water, they kept us company for about 2 miles when they left us,
because we were going too fast for them. St Paul's is better than the other
places on the Coast. It belongs to the Spaniards, about 1800 of which live
in the town, and about 3000 natives live in a separate town of huts. It is a
very dirty sort of place and the Spanish inhabitants such miserable-looking
creatures. There are always some Spanish gunboats in the harbour, and while
we were there a large Spanish man of war came in. I kept a diary for a few
days while we were in there so I will copy it on the next page, which will be
number eight.

December 29, 1879.

Turned out at 4 o'clock to keep the morning watch. Went ashore at 5.15
in the gig for provisions and to take the steward. Made fast off the bank
and cleaned out – then got the provisions on board. Steward came down
and we went on board. Spend forenoon doing nothing more or less. 1:30
pm went ashore with Miall in the cutter, which got aground half way
but easily got off again. Miall and I walked about the town going into
all the shops and humbugging all the Spanish and natives, walked up
the hill towards the Spanish barracks, passing on our way the prison,
the prisoners with their heads stuck out between the bars and having
baskets and other things made out of straw dangling from the windows
by pieces of string which they have made themselves and wanted to
sell. As there were no small things, and everything else was full of fleas
we bought nothing. We then went to some gardens where we saw a lot
of tiny little Portuguese boys dressed as dressed in soldier's uniform
and who called themselves the bandsmen. We then went on to an old
church which had evidently been burned down and they were now
restoring it. Amongst the ruins we saw these frightful old women. Two

of them were natives, the other half breed between a Portuguese and native. They looked just like three frightful old witches and they were working away collecting stones. We then came down and got into one of the chairs they carry you about in – I send you a rough sketch of one and I was carried to a shop. There I bought a shilling's worth of chocolate and some cakes, and then was conveyed down to the landing place where we found the cutter, manned by the racing crew waiting to pull us off and we got on board in a very short time. Then I kept my 6 to 8 watch and at 9 o'clock I lay down on the poop and was just going off to sleep when they sounded off to general quarters, so I turned in at 1030 very tired.

December 31 New Year's Eve.

Cleared lower deck at 6 o'clock, sent up to top gallant mast, crossed Royal yards. Kept the forenoon watch and kept the first watch 8–12pm so, it being New Year's Eve, at 1130 all the mids and clerks came up, except Williams who was asleep, and struggled manfully for the bell, for in the service it is considered a great thing to ring the old year out and the New Year in. I was fortunate in securing the tongue of the bell for myself from the Sentry for a quart of beer. So when at last the bell was hung up I got the first whack. The bell is supposed to be struck 15 times, but it must have been struck at least 25 times but I got a good share of it. I had about eight whacks and then after it was all over Williams came up with a flannel on his forehead – he had just been sleeping and could not make out at first what was up, but by degrees he began to understand that he had lost the chance of striking the old or new year out or in for 12 months. I then went down below into the gun room with the others, and we spent a remarkably jovial evening afterwards.

January 1st, New Year's day.

Went ashore at 7:00pm with the Chaplain. Dressed ship by request of Portuguese authorities. No difference was made on account of its being New Year's Day. We had an excellent dinner, and I send you the "Bill of Fare". We had a burning plum pudding and afterwards we sang many songs. I did not sing that night because I only know "Hearts of Oak" and "Ring the Bell, Watchman" and I only know those with the book.

January 5th Monday.

Commenced school again in the Captain's cabin. A large Portuguese man of war corvette arrived and anchored. Kept the middle watch during which I was lying down on the deck. As I was just going off to sleep a couple of monstrous rats ran over me, so up I jumped, I assure you. I don't think anybody could have jumped up so high and quickly from lying down fully stretched.

January 6 Tuesday 5:30 pm

Mail steamer *Mosquelle* arrived and anchored, but brought no letters for us. We were frightfully disappointed of course, but that was no use and at 10 o'clock weighed [anchor] and proceeded out of harbour under steam.

January 21, 1880 – St Helena.

We arrived here on Thursday evening last. We had a sweepstake about what time we should let go the anchor, and it was let go six minutes after my time. I was so disappointed. The prize was £1 and a ticket 2/6. I took up one & a half tickets, but as the whole ticket drew the time that was next to the real-time, I only had to pay 1/3. I send you some photos of the place, but now I must tell you that we got no letters when we came in last night, so the last letter I have got from home is dated October 15, 1879 a long time ago.

I went ashore on Sunday, it being my off day, with Chappell, the acting paymaster; at 12 o'clock we found our horses waiting for us, because Chappell had ordered them the night before (before I go any further I must tell you that I am very well and that we are going to the Cape of Good Hope tomorrow, Thursday) so we had some milk to drink at Scotts, the hotel, then mounted and rode up the hills. It was very monotonous going up the steep hills but at last we got up and then it was beautiful. We have splendid horses, the name of mine was 'Gang Forward' and Chapell's was 'Nimrod'. Mine was supposed to be the best horse in the island, it has won a great many races and it pulls like it! Nearly pulled my arms off. You would have laughed if you had seen me because I wore a pair of tight, tight breeches which Lindsay gave me a long time ago [and] they fitted me exactly. I was all about!!! Well we rode on, we galloped hard at every level place, till we came to a house called "Travellers Rest" where we met two of the Petty officers who wanted us to drink some of their beer but we refused. Chapel ordered a shandy gaffe (don't laugh at following) but I did not drink any of it because it was such frightfully bad beer, then we rode down into a valley to Napoleon's tomb. I send you the photo of it.

We had to sign our names in the book; then we rode up the other side to Longwood, a distance of about 1.5 miles, to see the Emperor's house. We did not see the house first but went into a little house where the First Lieutenant and Mr Ashworth were staying. They were very kind to me and us and gave us some sherry and biscuits and then took us to see some ostriches which belonged to the farmer. There were four male and two female, and he was farming them to sell their feathers which are beautiful. Then we went back to the house and then we mounted our horses and rode away father on towards a large flat plain of grass and furze where we had a fine gallop then we went off in the other direction till we came to another inn. When the landlord came to the door, he told us that the Captain had had breakfast there the day before so we thought if the place is good enough for the Captain it is good enough for us.

So we went in and ordered tea, which came in about 10 minutes, six boiled eggs, butter in heaps, honey, tea in gallons et cetera and fresh bread. It was a most delicious tea and we did justice to it because we had had no lunch: it was the first hard butter I had tasted since Madeira. We paid 2/6 each for the tea then we rode back to Longwood and went through the house. I send you the photo, it is very comfortable and all the rooms are on the ground floor, and on the second floor there are only attics in which his staff and servants used to sleep. Then he went to Baylies, the house where Mr Michaelson and Mr Ashworth are staying, and found that they had rode away to pay a visit to a farmer gentleman who had a lot of pretty daughters – but I being bashful!!! and tired, did not go, but lay down on the sofa and smoked one of Mr Michaelson's cigarettes and had a conversation with Bayley, and he showed me their rooms and a most delicious huge bath full of cold water. I could have had a bath only I was afraid that they might come while I was in the middle of it, and that would have been awkward – after Chapell came back and had some beer and I had a couple of glasses of delicious milk, then we remounted and galloped hard down to Scotts. The shoe off the left hind leg of my horse came off, making him a little lame, so that I had to get off and walk.

At Scotts we met Dr Atkinson and Lindsay, who had been onshore all day with the piquet, and we had some dinner and then we came on board at 8 o'clock and I was most frightfully tired and could hardly stand up or keep my eyes open in the morning watch. The next day I went ashore again with Miall but did not go for a ride but walked up to the top of the ladder, 699 steps, and went into the single station and had a chat with the old signalman. I watched the piquet down below chasing the noisy blue jackets. I gave him a shilling and we came away and went down the ladder very very much quicker than we went up. I meant to send you a photo of the ladder and town, but the fellow I asked to get them kindly forgot it. Well, when we got down again to Scotts we had tea, two poached eggs and three boiled each, cost 2/6 each. Then we walked about with Mr Roots and bought some things and came on board. Things are so awfully expensive – I paid for a straw hat, 4/6, a squash hat 4/6, handkerchiefs 2/6, work boots 4/– and several other things but they were all necessary articles. Then we came on board at 8 o'clock.

Today and yesterday it has been my watch so I could not go onshore. I don't think I ever told you a very important thing. We had our half yearly examinations and we all did very badly indeed,, but there is some excuse for me because I was sick for all that time you know. I was last but one out of the five … I didn't send you the papers because it would cost about sixpence and they would not interest you. We gave leave here, you know, and lots of the men have broken their leave and been drunk so I don't expect there will be much leave given at the Cape. We are off to the Cape tomorrow early and after we have spent about two months there we'll come up here again and spend three weeks here. The doctor is going ashore to advise that we should go on leave for about a week so I shall want some money, if you could send me some I should be very much obliged to you – the last bill I paid was for my washing so I can tell you that washing alone takes plenty of money out of my scanty pockets, however one thing I can say with a clear conscience that I owe no man a farthing! The Commodore left this place about a fortnight before we came in so we don't expect to meet him for some time.

Now I must tell you that I have had a slight accident the other day you know that my top two teeth are always painful and have been stopped about six times well my left back tooth was bothering me for some time so I bothered Dr Mitchell till he said he would pull it out. You may imagine it must have been pretty painful or else I would not have asked him to haul the back tooth out. When he asked me if it had been ever stopped so I like a fool did not remember exactly, so I told him that it had been stopped once, so he seated me on a chair, the sickbay man holding my head and he got a pair of tongs!!!, I mean tweezers and tugged at it for about 30 seconds and then, oh goodness, it snapped off just below the gum and it pains frightfully. The doctor looked at the tooth discovered at least 6 stoppings, so he was awfully angry with me and he was quite right. Now I am anxiously waiting for the gum to grow over it but it is but it pains very badly and I cannot touch it with anything. The tooth on the other side is also bothering me. I intend to go to a dentist at the Cape if there is a good enough one. I don't think though that I shall have any peace until I have all my back teeth out!!! Well, now I really must say goodbye I hope you will get this volume safe is a good thing because I don't think anybody ever wrote such an immense letter. I will send you a photo of the place and ladder next time we are there.

HMS *Dido* (at sea), February 1, 1880

The last letter I wrote to you was a pretty good long one, so I don't expect that this will be such a long one as it is composed mostly of what has happened since we have been at sea. I did not tell you about our poor painter, John Smith. We gave leave, you know, and the second day early in the morning a sergeant came off from the shore to tell us that he had found our painter dead under a wall. He had fallen over a wall on the cliff and fell onto another wall 10 feet below and broken his neck. He had been coming down the hill with the two other bluejackets all drunk. The two men who were with him did not know anything about it and when they came to their senses they found themselves in prison. So the next day the First Lieutenant, Mr Ashworth, Tawney and myself – officers, and a lot of blue jackets and a small arms party, went ashore to bury him. We have to wear our tail coats and swords.

Well, we started to go to the Dead House to get his body and I went in and looked at him before the lid was screwed down. I thought it was very horrible because his face was all bruised and cut. Then the coffin was put on a gun carriage drawn by a couple of good horses and we started up the hill. The whole way is about 4 miles, it seemed 20, and the height of the place above the level of the sea is 1700 feet, so you can imagine it was a walk! In full dress under a hot sun, the men stumbling because their boots were hurting them. Well, we buried him at the Cemetery and fired three volleys over him and came back again considerably faster than we went and I was dead tired. This was the day before I went ashore. There were a lot of other poor men's graves up there too. The country up there was awfully pretty, just like English scenery. On the way there Mr Michaelson got cramp in his leg so he escaped having to come the whole way.

And now I must jump to a different place altogether; halfway down to the long wished for Cape I have just sorted out the contents of my "ditty box", and everything in it reminded me of something nice that had taken place at home. That nice birthday book I looked through, it is in very good condition and several other little things which have been given to me by Papa and you and the others. I don't know if Maud remembers the little red pocketbook she gave me some time ago and she said she knew it would not be any use to me, well, she prophesied wrong because it has been most useful. I have made a Watch Bill in one end which I muster the watch and my division and the other end I use for sights and the other day taking sights. The Captain asked me if I had a bit of paper, so having none I gave him my little book so he worked out what he wanted to do in it and then gave it back and remarked that it was very neat little book! Please do tell Maud. We were going to take sights and then go off on the other tack to the Cape. But we are not going to do so and now we are steering straight to the Cape. We sighted and passed a large French frigate man of war, we saluted her with 11 guns and she returned the salute, she did look so nice firing, she was about 3 miles off. The smoke hid her from view after she fired.

A few nights ago at 12 o'clock we had night quarters and fired two broadsides, blank cartridges, it was a pitch dark night, the guns going off looked so nice. I lay on my coat with my pillow under my head and in my clothes with my Dirk lying by my side, because we have to lash our hammocks close up so when the bugle went at 1130 I was all ready, instead of lashing up my hammock while all the men were getting theirs stowed alongside of my hammock. The thermometer is so nice and low, last night it showed 63° [17°C]. I wear a big coat in the night watch now because it is very cold. I expect to have plenty of delicious grapes at the Cape. The First Lieutenant and Lindsay have both been sick for some time so I expect they will soon go home. The other day we gave two of the Wardroom offices a dinner, which came off very successfully. I send you the bill of fare that I retrieved. I forgot to send you the skin of my animal in my last mail so I must try and remember to send it next send it this time.

February 7, 1880 (at sea)

Here we are still at sea. 16 days have we been out at sea and expect to remain five more before we get into Simons Bay. We are now flying along at the rate of 8 knots, right before the wind and have not got all sails set because it is too strong a breeze. We are accompanied during the day by two different kinds of birds, the noble albatross and the small Cape pigeon. The albatross is such a beautifully big bird but we have not seen any real big ones yet. These that occasionally fly round the ship measure about 7 feet from the tip of the wings. You can catch them with a hook and a piece of meat towing astern but we are afraid that the Captain will say something. Now I must leave writing on this fancy piece of paper, so goodbye for some moments because I am immediately going to commence writing on another piece of paper.

HMS *Dido* (at Sea)

Chart of track between St Helena and Simon's Bay by B. G-F.

From St Helena to Simon's Bay, February 7th 1880

The other day I was asked into the wardroom to dinner with some others. I had a very nice dinner and sat next to Dr Atkinson, who is very nice to me as he has always been.

(Feb 12) So now I will go on from where I have left off above. We are at present snugly anchored in Simon's Bay and I have been round the Cape of Good Hope so I can stick one leg on the table. I will be able to stick the other one on the table after I have been round Cape Horn. The other day before we came in we saw such a beautiful albatross, such a big one too. The Captain tried to shoot some with his pistol but missed. There were about 10 of them flying about the ship. The last few days of the journey we were obliged to have fiddles[19] when we had anybody to dinner. The Wardroom and Captain and I use them always because things used to roll off. We used to have nothing on the table except our plates and knives and forks then when we wanted water we could not let the glass be out of your hand for a minute. We gave another dinner to the Wardroom and had Dr Mitchell and Mr Root (Dr and engineer). In the middle watch at sea I always used to use at least one pot of cocoa, making nice hot cocoa for the officer of the watch and to some of the petty officers. We also gave, a few nights after the dinner mentioned above, a dinner to the Warrant Officers, the Gunner and Bosun, and now I will begin another letter answering your letters and telling you that what news there is since we received the mail.

The mail steamer does not come into Simon's Bay, it anchors off Cape Town and the letters are sent overland to Simon's Town. We came into this place with a rattling breeze so it was blowing too hard for us to pick up our moorings so we let go both our anchors. Early this morning we up anchored and took our moorings. Now I think I'll begin about the letters I received from you all. The letters I received and which were waiting for me were as follows (I received no November letters so I expect they are on the coast somewhere) and now I will read all the ones through and answer them as I go in order. I hope you will be able to get Colmore to stay with you. I do not know his address or I would write to him, he is very jolly and lively. I may as well tell you he likes lots to do … But he is so awfully nice I'm sure you will like him.

I had such an awfully nice letter from uncle Robert, you know I sent him a photo of the ship he seemed so thankful for it … I am glad you were interested in my poor account of the palavers in the Bonny. Were the Christmas presents under the tablecloth, the same they were last Christmas? What a lot of Christmas cards you all got. Is it nice having a pew up in the gallery at the Parish? I feel greatly honoured by you all drinking my health on Christmas day. I have no doubt that you were surprised at finding my silver in the parcel but the history of it is as follows – when Colmore was sent to the *Dwarf* he had not got his silver complete or something so he asked me to lend him mine, so of course I did and when he joined us again he did not bring it back with him but left it in the *Dwarf* till we should meet her, but he met her on the way home in the mail boat and took them both with him and sent them to the same address as the other things. I can't make out about your not receiving the other things because I put them all in his chest myself, but he must have forgotten it. I wish I could have sent more curios in the dressing case but the truth is I

---

19 mall wooden bars around the edges of the table tops

had no more. We are almost certain not to be sent to the Mediterranean after this station. I believe it is said we are going to relieve the *Danae* at Australia, a most delicious station and letters every week. If the things I wrote for us are sent at once I'm certain to get them. How very sad it is about that railway accident in Scotland. That animal I saw floating on the top of the water going into the Bonny was not a sea serpent but a fish as I afterwards found, seeing some near me.

I'm sorry you had not a good time shooting at Sherborne, I know the cover[20] you mean well. I'm so glad you got the woodcock. It was very kind of the shooting party to ask about me. I hope Mr Bathe and Mr Walwyn are getting on well. I am so much obliged to you for telling me I need not stamp the letters, it will save me a small sum. I'm very much obliged to you for the dear little present of the tooth of the first shark I ever saw set in gold. It is so pretty, Papa, I shall wear it on my watch chain. I like it much better than a pin. My watch is safe in my ditty box only the weather has put it out of order. I'm going to take it to a jeweller if there is one here but there is sure to be one at Cape Town. Remember me to Mr Stansfield, please. He is very kind to be asking about me so often. I shall look forward to getting the parcel and looking in it and seeing what things you have sent me, Mother, it will be like examining a hamper.

Royal Naval Club, Simons Bay, February 16, 1880

I will now go on writing to you this letter (separate) ought to be read before this. I wish with all my might that you win the next prize for acrostics; what hard luck you're not getting the last one. I have just been to pay a long visit to the First Lieutenant and Lindsay who are both in hospital here. Is it not good of me, hating visiting as I do? I think they will both be out of it very soon. Captain Parr is coming down soon to see Lindsay. I came ashore this morning and have been looking about. I bought a tie and have just come in and have ordered tea for 5. 45. I will tell you what the two of us are going to have (Chapell and myself) – you must take into consideration that we have had no luncheon though – six chops, six poached eggs on toast, four boiled eggs fresh bread, butter, tea, milk and sugar and salt and pepper, a pretty good tea, don't you agree with me. Better even than the one we had last night. I have just written to Uncle Robert. I don't know if I told you I won a sweepstake, 17/6, but I think I did. I don't think there's anything else of consequence to tell you. We were exactly 20 days on our passage from St Helena to here without

---

20 specific small area for a shoot to take place

sighting land. Yesterday we all came ashore to church, the first time I have been to church onshore for more than six months. Love to all

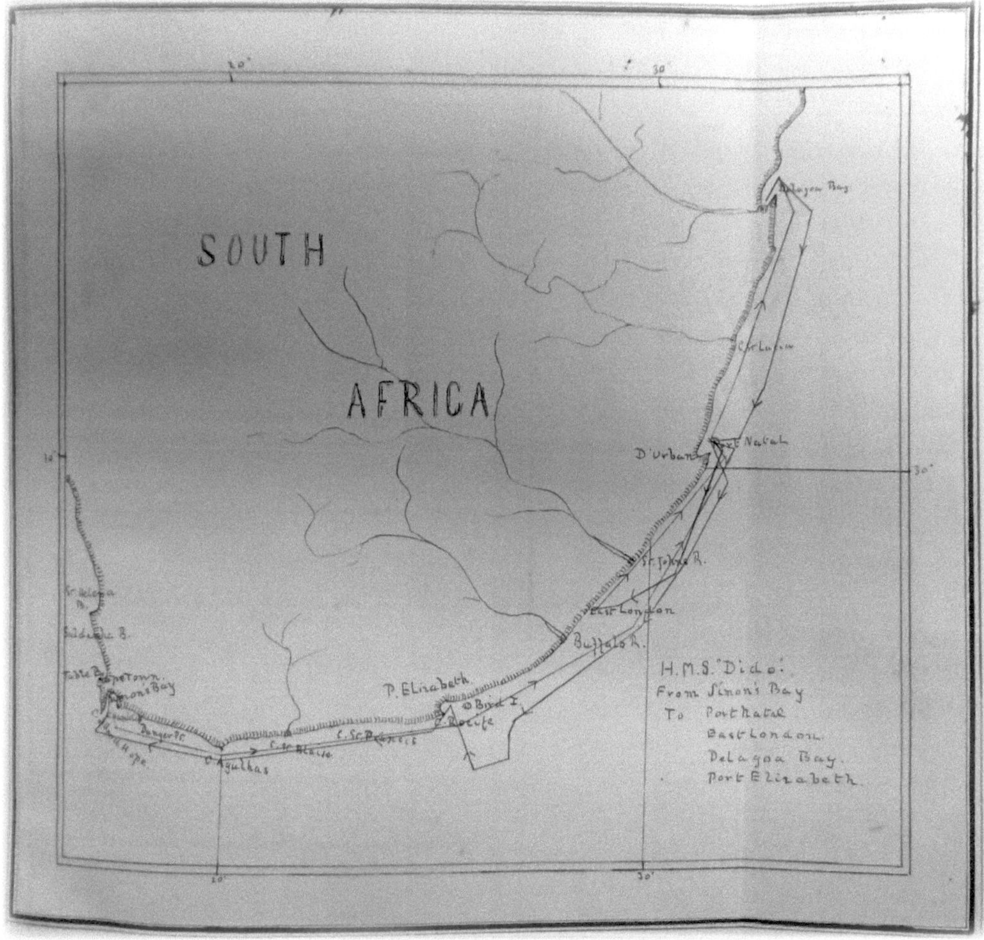

Chart of South Africa, drawn by B.G-F.

HMS *Dido*, Simons Bay, March 1, 1880

I am so very sorry that I did not send my letter to you by the last mail but I could not because I couldn't post it. I will tell you why. I went ashore with Williams the day the mail was supposed to go, intending to come on board to post my letter but as you will see I could not. We went to the Club and read and smoked and played billiards, wrote my letter, and had an extra prodigious tea. At 6:30 pm after tea we went down to the pier to try to get a boat off (it was blowing hard) but there was no one down there, so we went to the boatman's house and he told us he would not take us off on any account because he was certain he could not get back again, so then we were onshore and not able to get off to the ship, so we went and engaged a bedroom at the hotel with two very nice beds in. At the hotel we met a fellow called Case who had been a midshipman in the service long ago and we went out humbugging with him. Then we turned in at 9.30 and went to sleep.

The next morning Williams woke me up at 4.30, so I dressed, as the wind had gone down. We went and woke the boatman up and he took us off to the ship. Then I turned in and slept till 6.30, and we got into no row because of course it was not our fault, but anyhow I was not able to post the letter. I was in a dreadful state of mind because I received no letters from home this mail,, only one from Cousin Alfred. I would like you, if it is no trouble, to mark what the thermometer is in your letter. It is from 64 to 74 here during the 24 hours and it is nearly always blowing five days out of the five. I took the skin of the animal I told you about some time ago to the post office the other day and I discovered that it would cost five shillings to send it home so I thought I will keep it and take it home myself …

I was very unfortunate the other day. I have had £2.12 shillings stolen so I am afraid I cannot go and enjoy myself up at Cape Town yet. The other day we played against another ship in cricket and got beaten. I umpired for two innings and after I had umpired I went to the First Lieutenant at the hospital. I like him very much and he was just going out for a drive, so he asked me to come with him so I said yes so I had a very jolly long ride. I sent him and Lindsay books and papers and I am going soon to fish for him because he's only allowed to eat fish principally. Nicholson has gone on a few days leave to Cape Town so we are in three watches which is very hard work … I hope all the dear ones at home and in Ireland are well and enjoying the cold. I hope I'll get a letter from you next mail. There are going to be some theatricals tomorrow night on shore, our blue jackets are going to act. I don't know whether I am going. I probably won't be able to get onshore because there will be a watch to keep I expect, and now goodbye because I have to go to the next letter, a better one than this.

HMS *Dido*, Simons Bay, March 7, 1880

The other day I got out my photo album from the First Lieutenant's cabin and looked at it over and over again. I wish you could send me some of anybody I know, or any relation I don't know, I like them so much. I will give you a list

of those I really want … Aunt Emy wrote such a nice letter and sent me a very
nice photograph of Teddy, and I also got one from dear old uncle George who
sent me a lock of Rose's hair off her left ear. Please thank him for her hair and
letter and Aunt Emmy for the photo. I am going to write to them as soon as
possible.

I will now tell you something a little more cheerful because I daresay it will
amuse you. On Saturday last the Captain called me into his cabin and after a
little talk he said he would want me to go off in charge of our steam cutter and
tow his galley with himself and the two Miss Freres (Sir Bartle's daughters)
out to a lighthouse, so I did so and got very wet because it was very rough, and
then he asked me to go to lunch with them, Mr Ashworth, the Chaplain, and
the two Miss Freres. The next day, Sunday, came and the Captain called me
up and told me he would want me to go away on the galley, (a great honour to
go) and go inshore to the Commodore's pier and walk up to the Commodore's
house where the Miss F's are staying and see if they were ready. So up I went
and was shown into a charming drawing room kind of affair (otherwise a lot of
rooms opening into one another) where Mrs Richards (C.'s wife) and the Miss
F.'s were, so I sat down on a sofa, the depth of which I was nearly drowned,
and talked away like anything and was not a bit shy. Mrs Richards is very nice,
she is an invalid, and she asked me to go and see her very often. So they went
out and got ready and Mrs Richards and myself had a great tête-à-tête and
when they came back we walked down to the boat and went on board, where
the Captain and the officers of the watch received them and took them into his
Cabin, so I ran down to put on my white waistcoat and went up to lunch.

Well, after lunch I went down to the gun room and at about 3.10 went up
and took them onshore again in the galley and walked with them through the
gardens up to the house, where I went in and looked at some of their sketches,
and then they asked me to go up and have lunch with Lady Frere near Cape
Town and all that kind of thing. And that I should see Major Parr and that Lady
Frere held her receptions on Thursday if I'd liked to go up on that day et cetera
et cetera. I wish you would make me a present of a book called Sketches in
the Hunting Field, as it is taken from the 'Sp. and Draw'. I have read a few of
them and the illustrations in this book are going to be new and I should like it
very much. I send you the newspaper cutting about it, only send it by post and
mind it has the illustrations please. I have not been ashore since I wrote to you
last mail, except on duty.

I am so awfully sorry that Mr Michaelson is going home, it is not certain
but it is more than probable. We are allowed to bathe on board in the morning
only we have not done so yet because it is too cold. The other day I saw a

small shark, only the sharks here I believe are not supposed to eat people.
I suppose you have seen that picture of Lord Ramsay and his wife in the
Graphic, about some political business. It is exactly like him but very bad
of his wife. I'm writing this letter at 1 o'clock in the middle of the night, it is
my middle watch and I'm writing in the gun room at the risk of the Captain
coming out and skinning me. The letters go tomorrow morning, rather this
morning. I only got one Christmas card and that was from Cousin George,
one of those De la Rue funny ones. That account of Admiral Fanshawe's
retirement was very interesting. What a lot of nice parties you were having at
home about Christmas time, quite gay. Please give my love to Miss Walwyn's
mother and tell her I will write to her, I will write as soon as I can find time.
Last Sunday we all went to Church in the dockyard, they have services in a
sail loft, just the table and pulpit are screened off from the rest of the room.
During the week our chaplain has to go onshore, because the dockyard one is
sick. Now I must say goodbye but love to all.

Royal Naval Club, Simon's Town, March 14, 1880

Thanks very much for your nice letter and the Cheque for £5. There is not
much to tell you. I have been to see Mr Michaelson once since I wrote to you
last week and I believe there is a chance of his coming on board again very
soon. I received a letter from F &.D advising me that the gear was coming by
the *Orontes*. I hope it will be soon because I believe I am going to stay with
Lady Frere at Government House – hmmm! Hmmm!! Hmmm!!! The Captain
is away now and we are having splendid times on board …

And now I will answer your letter. I hope, Mother, that your neuralgia has
quite gone and won't come back again!!! I am so glad you are giving such
a number of afternoon parties, you must all enjoy them so much. Have you
got Colmore to stay with you? He would like them very much, I think. Thank
Cousin Cecil as hard as you can for his kindness about the present, I will
think as soon as I can what I would like. I really would like to write to him if
I could, but after I have written this letter I must go and see Mr Michaelson
and Lindsay. The opening of Parliament must have been a grand sight from all
accounts.

The only other person in the reading room besides myself, at present, is a
parson, I don't know him (is not that interesting?).

I hope Cousin Nellie is quite well again now. Remember me to Cousin
Harriet, but of course she is gone ages ago. Thanks very much for the
newspaper cuttings … The tooth of Hilda that you, Papa, sent me I never

got. I saw a little hole in the bottom of the envelope so I suppose that some inquisitive beggar had taken it out. I am so sorry because it might have filled in a place where mine was hauled out. Thanks very much, mother, for the Eau de Cologne and little book and that are coming in the *Orontes*. I will use them I promise you, and if my tooth is bad the medicine. I don't think that there is any dentist here that I would like to trust my magnificent teeth to!! The parson has just gone so I can breathe better. I have just taken a walk out onto the veranda and found our Gunnery Lieutenant snoring in an armchair. I hope for the credit of the *Dido*-dum that nobody sees or hears him. I am getting on capitally at billiards. My plain clothes are beginning to look shabby. it is uncertain which station we will probably go to, the West Indies or Australia. I am so glad to hear Maxwell is getting on well, is it impossible for him to be an officer? I am quite well and have not been sick (even seasick) since I left England. I hope Miss Hartland is better, please give her my love. You tell me that May B. has got two godfathers, Morris Wall and Cousin Alfred. Now I always thought that a female (beg pardon) could only have one godfather and two godmothers and a male (beg pardon) two godfathers and one godmother.

And now my darlings all, I think I must say adieu because there is nought more to say. I hope you will send me that book I asked for you for in my last letter, 'Sketches in the Hunting Field', if you can. We have had quite fine weather lately. Best love to all the dear sisters and brothers and the Irish ones.

HMS *Dido*, Simons Bay, March 27, 1880

Thanks for nice long letter: you will think that I am beginning to be irregular about writing but I am *not*. The last time I missed the mail because I was on shore, and they sent the bag sooner than usual because it was coming on to blow and I could not send anybody on shore to post it at, as it was blowing so hard. What an awfully nice little picture that is of Maud; when I first saw it I was not sure that she had cut the picture out of the book or photographed it, which latter I think she must have done. And now I will begin to answer your letter. I hope Cousin Harriet is better; it will be nice to change into another house for a time but I hope you will go back to the old home in the square afterwards. How pretty the christening of May Bee must have been and how kind of Cousin A. I give her the CS[?]. They are acting *HMS Pinafore* up in Cape Town, I shall try and go and see if I can get leave for a night because Cape Town is 22 miles off and if you like you can get a pass from a certain Major down there which enables you to see Cetewayo [?] for Naval officers. Thanks so much for all the gear, I received all safely. Thank Cousin's A and G for the nice presents. I will write and thank them when I have time – I think that I should like Cousin Cecil [to] give me a nice silver watch chain, but I would rather have the 10 shillings. I'm sorry to say that my time is up at the Club. I have been an honorary member for six weeks paying 2/6 per week and now I must either go or become a life member which means paying 30/– more. There is no other place on shore where you can go to which is very unfortunate and I'm getting on so well with billiards. A fellow beat me a short time ago by 10 in the game of 50 and yesterday I played him two games of 100 each, the first time I beat him by eight and the second time when I was game he was 63. I'm very fond of it.

The Sunday before this Captain Domvile sent me ashore to get some more ladies, only this time they were all out at Church. Thanks so much for the photo of Aunt Beatrice that you sent me it is such a very nice one and looks so well in my book. Please give her my love. Dear nice Mr Michaelson our First Lieutenant is going home at last. I am so frightfully sorry … He has given me his bath, a very nice one. I went to see him and Lindsay again yesterday. Lindsay is better, he will soon be out of hospital and on-board again I expect. My plain clothes are awfully shabby the Captain noticed them the other day. He says that all the Gunroom officers clothes are shabby. Cool! We have had beautiful weather lately, no more S.E'ters for ages. I like the little book you sent me, Mother, so much. I remember some of the things in it are the same as those I used to read with you. The *Moutito* troopship was in here the other day for a few days and landed the wives and children of some soldiers at Natal. The Captain told me and Bruce to go to one of Lady Frere's receptions and we were going last week but as it was Passion Week we did not go, we are sure to go soon though; I don't like it a bit. I was thinking of having my photograph taken at Cape Town, there is a very good photographer there but I don't think I shall because I cannot afford it. I would give anything to be going home with the First Lieutenant. He has offered to take any gear home for me. I shall see if I can't send anything. A hamper of fruit I think would be nice if it would keep! Lots of grapes et cetera,. would you like it? There is going to be a prizes given for the best 64lb er, and the cleanest one of the guns in my quarters have the best chance of getting it. The other day all the blue jackets went ashore rifle shooting at the target and the Captain and myself went and we fired at the target. First we fired at 300 yards. The marks are as follows. Bulls eye 4, centre 3, outer 2, and out of 10 shots I got 17, with one bull's-eye, the Captain got 17 no bull's-eye. Then we fired again and he was better and I was not so good. Then we went to 100 yards out of the same number of shots as the Captain I got 2 bull's-eye's, both of them better than the bulls eyes, that I got, so I am not a bad shot!!! The other day I and two others drove 15 miles away in a hired car. We had great fun. I gave the boy 2/- to let me drive and I made them (pair of horses) go along at a spanking rate. We got on board at 9 o'clock. We went to see Admiral Etheridge, but as he was out we saw a friend who was staying in the house and then we went and saw an awfully good fellow Carr who used to be a mid in the Navy and was to be one of the wildest fellows going, he is a man now. Yesterday I was asked to ashore the whole day. I went and played in a scratch match and our side beat, then I went and bathed and had a good tea at the Club. Then I came on board and read your letter. The other day I went to play lawn tennis in the Commodore's garden but we only had one game because there were some drains which smell horribly. Give my best love to all the darling ones in Rockenham and elsewhere and remember me to Miss Walwyn and Miss Hartland. I'm afraid darlings that there is no more to say. I'm sending you a few of these pretty leaves. The First Lieutenant came off on board today and lunched with the Captain. Thanks for the writing paper.

Cogills Hotel Wynberg, April 5, 1880

I am on leave. The Captain was very nice, he said to me that Williams and myself had better go on leave otherwise we will not be able to go at all, because the Commodore would be coming back, and he said that we might go and stay at Cogill's Hotel from Monday to Thursday, so I nearly fell down with joy. The idea of being out of the ship for a few days was delicious, so the Captain gave us a lift up here in his trap, he is going to stay here till Wednesday; we have just come up, this place is 16 miles from Simon's Town. We intended to walk it, only the Captain offered us the lift. We have just had dinner. I have brought up my uniform and white waistcoat because we are going with the Captain to a dance given by some tremendous big swells at a place called Claremont, and the next night we are going to the theatre to see a piece called "The Two Roses". I don't believe it is up to much, they have just left off having "Pinafore".

I must now tell you about the swell Wednesday. On Wednesday last we invited the Governor, Sir Bartle Frere and all the Ministers and their several ladies (if they had any) on board to see us fire off a 100lb. torpedo. Well, as luck would have it, it was a thundery blowing day, but anyhow they all came on board and after they had fired off the torpedo which sent the water as high as the topsail yard that sounded off the General Quarters, so of course I, the aide-de-camp, had to go up on the poop next to the Captain and amongst all the people. Well the Captain called me and whispered that he wanted to present me to the Governor, so I was presented with all due form and had a long chat with His Excellency and two or three more afterwards; he is

an awfully nice old fellow and said he hoped he would often see me up at
Government House et cetera et cetera, then the Captain introduced me to Miss
Frere, who I had been introduced to before. They asked me to go and stay with
them and Captain Parr also asked me to write and say when I was coming. I
had long chats with some of the funny old Ministers; you can imagine what
a swell I looked in my new dirk and tail coat!!! And then in the evening they
went away and the Governor shook hands with me (a great honour) when he
was going.

On Saturday last I came up here with our eleven, made up of the Naval and
Military in Simon's Bay to see the match against the Western Province (and
I saw a fellow called Gray who used to be the Captain of the first eleven at
Fosters), and we beat them; in the middle of the day I went up by train to Cape
Town and went to see Major Parr at Government House but he had just gone
out to some other place and then I got measured for a new suit of plain clothes,
because the Captain told me that mine are getting shabby. All the clothes were
awfully expensive so I got one of the cheaper ones (serge) and he said he
would send the bill home £3/17s. I also bought some Zulu curiosities for you
which I have just sent home by the First Lieutenant – a Zulu necklace. If you
smell it you will find that it certainly belonged to a native because it has got a
decidedly native smell, which I know well by this time, and a Zulu pipe which
is hewn out of a piece of stone. I would have brought a lot more curiosities,
but they were so very expensive and you must not mind if I say that it is my
Christmas present to you all. I would have brought you another necklace made
of Tigers teeth only they wanted £1 for it. Also an ostrich feather (a beauty) for
16/- and a couple of ostrich eggs for 3/-, only they will be such a bother to the
first lieutenant to take. I will send you the eggs if I can have them packed up
neat enough only I don't know if you would care for them. I'm going up there
again tomorrow and I will see if there's anything more.

I will have lots of news to tell you next mail, all about the dance et cetera.
Captain Domvile is going to take Williams and myself to see King Cetewayo
and his wives tomorrow, is not that jolly? Now you have something to brag
about!!! I am so awfully sorry dear Mr Michaelson is going home tomorrow in
the mail steamer. I shall go and see him off, he is very ill; and now my hand is
really tired.

I will answer your letter first. I have had such a nice letter from dear
Rockenham, such an exciting story about dear aunt Jet and about dear
Granny's cow "Queen Dido". I am sure I hope she will like her Dido better
than I like my *Dido*! I hope dear dear Aunt Edie will soon get a nice dog.
Please tell darling Granny that I will write to her next mail, as she wants one of

my long letters, so I will not write to you, but will tell her all the news and she will send the letter on to you.

I hope you enjoyed your visit to Plymouth, mother, I am so glad Miss Hartland is well again. Remember me kindly to Miss Walwyn and Kate. I'm glad you are going to make the nursery your bedroom, it is much nicer. I am so glad you are not going to leave old number 18. And now darlings goodbye and love to you all and those in Ireland, I'm just going to have a game of billiards with Williams before going to bed.

Royal Naval Club, Simon's Town, April 11, 1880

I have just eaten four mutton chops and three eggs, and smoked one cigarette and I now sit down intending to write to a very long letter as it is nice and quiet. First of all since I last conversed with you on paper I have shaken hands with royalty and stayed with the height of society, in other words I have shaken hands with his Majesty King Cetewayo and stayed with Sir Bartle Frere. I will now tell you all about it. When I last wrote to you it was from Cogill's hotel. Well, after I had written to you I went and turned into my bed. I and Williams had a very large nice room between us and I slept like a top. (The Captain has just come into the room and I was just too late to get under the table.)

The next morning we were down to 8.45 breakfast, after which we started with the Captain up to Cape Town. First we went to the 'Old Curiosity Shop' where I bought the Zulu necklace and pipe which I have not been able to send you, but the Captain bought nothing there. Then we went to the Castle, and here the Captain enquired for Colonel Hazard and after a short chat with him we went towards Cetewayo's apartments; it was fortunate for us that he was well that morning otherwise we would not have seen him, because sometimes when he is seedy he stays in bed. But the Colonel having found out from the interpreter that he was out on the battlement, we walked up some narrow stairs and then along a flat place with sentries posted every here and there, and we saw one of the native maids and a Zulu man (Cook), who was perfectly naked all except the small skin they wear, and he had the brass ring on his head which you see in pictures. Well, we went up for a few more stairs till we came to the top of the fort onto a kind of battlement with the big guns and sentries all round – and seated near one of the guns on a native mat with a cloak wrapped round him was old Cetewayo, and close to him were two of his chiefs or attendants.

I forget their names, they were huge big men, only one of them had a Scotch cap on and a big coat, and I forget what the other one had but the old beast with the Scotch cap had a long kind of ivory knife affair with which he continually scooped out his nose and eyes and then wiped it on his hand. Well we talked to him (Cetewayo) through the interpreter and asked him how he was. The poor old fellow is very seedy, and the Colonel told him that I was going to be an Admiral some day at which the three of them laughed long and heartily, and then we all shook hands with him and he nearly shook my hand off he gave it such a shake.

Then we went on our way down again, where we saw his four wives seated by another gun making straw spoons, which they mix the native beer with, and they all were laughing and talking as if they were very happy. They are very good looking for Negro women as they were – they did not wear drapes but wore their own Zulu garments, two of them had their hair done in such a funny way all stuck up something like only more on top of their heads it looked all stuck together and crystallised. Then we said goodbye to them. The only English words that Cetewayo and the others can say are "Good bye".

We saw his apartments, it is nearly 3 dormitories in one big room, one of which is his reception room and *all* of which *smell horribly*. I bought a photo of him in the same cloak and sitting on the same mat as I saw him, and I bought one of one of his ugly wives without her hair done up, the only one I could find, and with two little natives on her lap. I recognised her photo soon after I

King Cetewayo.

One of King Cetewayo's wives.

A Zulu warrior in
'undress uniform'.

came out, in a shop window. Well as soon as we came out the Captain left us so we went on and had some ices, bought some white gloves for the dance, ties and a few other things, and then we went to the City Club – all Naval Officers are honorary members of it – and had lunch and played a 50 and 63 game of billiards, in the latter of which game I beat Williams.

Then we walked down to the dockyard to the Glantully Castle to see dear Mr Michaelson off. Well, he had not yet arrived, so having met the Captain there we all sloped about looking all over her and a beautiful steamer she is, one of the Donald Currie line which used to call at Dartmouth. Well, soon Mr. Michaelson came on board with the doctor and one or two others who had come to see him off, and we had a little chat with him and then we heard the bell go. I said goodbye to him and asked him to remember me to Mr Guy Mainwaring in the Britannia who used to be so kind to me, and I declare I could only just prevent myself from shedding a bitter tear because he really was so very kind to me. He told me that I had better pack myself up in an envelope and go with him, and indeed I wish I could because I should then have seen all your dear old faces again!!! Well, we waited on the jetty so as to see the last of him, then the beautiful ship steamed out of the dock with our dear First Lieutenant, whom I suppose I should never have the pleasure of seeing again. He asked me to send him one of my photographs as soon as I could and he is going to send me one of his, so just send me out a few of the kind I liked, please. If I had enough money I would have my photo taken here because there is a very good photographer here. I will be able to try my new suit of clothes tomorrow,. The Captain says he is very glad I'm having a new suit made.

Well, [we] having seen the last of our no longer First Lieutenant, a man called Mr Hanson, an awfully jolly fellow, took us (Captain Domvile, Mr Atkinson, Williams and myself) to the Civil Service Club to quench our thirst, after which we went down to Wynberg by train and Capt. D.W. and self went to dress for dinner with Sir Bartle Frere at the Vineyards. When we were dressed we got into the vehicle which was to take us and drove to the Vineyard (the place where the Frere's stay in summer time). Well, we went in that very jolly drawing room and then we went into dinner. At dinner there was besides Capt Domvile, Williams and myself, Sir Bartle Frere, Mr Lyttleton's private secretary, Major Parr, Mr Dalrymple, his aide-de-camp and three Miss Frere's and Lindsay. I was placed next to the Governor and Mr Dalrymple, and I had a very nice dinner. There were three footmen waiting, and I had a chat about politics and other affairs with Sir Bartle. He is an awfully nice man.

Next day, after lunch, we had a game of lawn tennis and looked at the horses and two dear little deer and dogs. Then they asked us to stay with them and go to a lawn tennis party at 4 o'clock, and after that to go to a children's fancy dress ball and then to sleep there till next day. So of course I said yes, but Williams said no and yes and at last he said yes, so they said they could only put me up for the night as there was not another room. So Williams decided to go back to Cogill's after the ball because he wanted to walk down next morning early. So I went to the station and telegraphed for my things and then we came back, and as there was not room in the carriage we walked to the lawn tennis place and had a game of tennis. Then we went back again to the Vineyard where we discovered Lady Frere had come back and the other Miss Frere, so we just dressed again, and there and then the first part of us went to this place to the fancy ball. I went in the carriage the second time with Sir Bartle and Lady Frere and Miss Frere, so you see I had good company!

Well when we got there I was introduced to and danced three dances with the prettiest girl in the room, the daughter of the Dutch Consul. There were about 200 children there altogether and all dressed in the sweetest and most perfect dresses I ever saw, in fact it was the prettiest sight I ever saw and am ever likely to see. There were tiny little children, like dear little Hilda, with sweet fancy dress, a Beefeater and one little thing like a baby in a lady's dress of the 18th-century with powdered hair. I enjoyed it immensely. Sir Bartle, with all his orders on and in uniform, went round speaking to nearly all the little children, but to explain it all properly I should be talking to you (sitting in a chair between Papa and Mother), it is useless telling you on paper. I may as well tell you that the host and hostess were French people. There were those big paper lamps hung on the trees outside, it was so pretty. Well, we came away rather soon, I am sorry to say, so I said goodbye to my sweet partner who was dressed as a Spanish peasant. We drove back and had dinner, this time at dinner there was Sir Bartle and Lady Frere, Mr. Dalrymple, Lindsay and the four Miss Frere's, so after dinner we went into the drawing room and looked at books and one thing and another, and then having said good night we went to turn in (they had got Williams to stay).

So the next morning I was down in good time for prayers, and after breakfast I said goodbye to Sir Bartle and Lady Frere. Both of them asked me if I could not stay longer and to come and stay when ever I could. I thanked them very much, and then I went and said goodbye to Miss Frere and had to write my name in the book and was asked to send my photo as soon as I could get one, so please send me two or three; and then, my bag being packed, I got into an awfully jolly little pony cart which Mr. Dalrymple had kindly lent me, and Lindsay and I drove down to Wynberg where we paid a visit to Admiral

Etheridge, and then Lindsay left me at Cogills and he went on again. I shifted into plain clothes at Cogill's and then went up to Cape Town where I spent two hours and tried on my new coat, and then I came down to Cogill's, paid my bill and drove down in the mail cart to Simon's Town having enjoyed my leave thoroughly.

Nothing particular has happened since then, so now I must stop as my fingers are aching, and I have had my joke at the Cape and spent all my money except for one shilling. I will write my next letter home to granny; give my best love to all the darling ones at home and in Ireland. I received a letter from dear Nora and Maud this last mail. I send you two packets of seeds; they must not be kept hot, mind. The *Raleigh* is expected daily.

HMS *Dido* at sea – from Saldanha Bay to St Helena, May 29, 1880

We have left nice Simons Bay, I'm sorry to say, and we went to Saldanha Bay, only about 60 miles away. There are only a few huts in Saldanha Bay but it is a splendid place for shooting. The Captain and our new Chaplain, Mr Nicholls, went away shooting the first and second day we were there. We were only there two days and on the first day they shot two bucks and one partridge and the second day they shot three bucks, one partridge and one pigeon; the bucks are such dear little things, they are about the size of a large greyhound. Well it was my turn to land the first day, so I got my gun and as many cartridges as I could collect and Williams shouldered his gun, and we all got into the cutter, intending to land on an island where there were any amount of rabbits, but as nobody knew the proper place we were landed at the wrong island, where there was not a single rabbit, only a lot of seagulls and herons and other large seabirds. Well, the cutter had gone too far away when we discovered that it was the wrong island, so we had to stay there for about six hours. We amused ourselves as best we could buy shooting the birds. I shot one enormous bird like an albatross. It was an awfully good shot! I was sitting behind a rock when I saw him flying past over my head so I jumped up quickly and fired and he fell down into the water. I had not killed, only wounded him because of course he was such a big chap, so as he was struggling in the water I thought he might swim away so I fired at him again and killed him and then the wind blew him right in so I took off my boots and socks and went in after him. I also killed two big black birds (shags): like ducks, which were flying away from me. Of course I missed a great many birds because I only fired at them when they were flying, simply because I could not get close to any while I was sitting. It was very good practice was it not! I chased a very pretty bird with a bent beak, just like a heron and with black tips to his wings round the island twice but I could only get one shot at him and I missed that. There were also some pigeons, but they flew a great deal too fast for me. I'm having the wings of the big bird prepared as I am going to try and send them home. When I stretched the wings out after I had shot him I should think they measured a little more than 4 feet from tip to tip. There was also a small hut on the island with a few ships names in it so I made *Dido* in about twice as large letters as any other ship. I fired off one cartridge in it and I thought the walls of the hut we going to fall in on me. Well, the next day I could not go as I had to look out for the watches.

In the morning of the next day we came out, and now we are on our way to St Helena. I was greatly flattered when just before the ship sailed from Simons Town our Captain came on board, having been to Cape Town, and told me that Lady Frere wished to be kindly remembered to me. I have not sent them a photo yet. I think I shall wait till we go to Simons Bay, then if I can afford it I shall have my photo taken and then I can send them one.

We shall soon have to shut our ports and then the gunroom will be very hot and nearly dark. I have got a few more silver leaves that I am sending you. I am making an awfully jolly scrapbook, mixing newspaper cuttings and nice horsey pictures all up together. Please send me any newspaper cuttings that say anything about anyone we know or the Rockenhamers know. And now I must stop, the ship is beginning to roll horribly so I must wait till a more convenient opportunity. Goodbye for the present (we had a small skylight cut over our heads, so it admits both the air and light which is very nice).

At sea– about three days off St Helena

I really don't know what to say to you. At St Helena if I can, and if we see the *Humber*, I'm going to have a box made and send home some things (curiosities, those wings and the skins: I wonder what it is like now). Nothing interesting has happened since I last wrote. Mr Nicholls told me late last night I had worked very well with him as yet. I like him because I feel as if he was really teaching me something. I intend to have a day's riding at St Helena if I can manage it. I'm looking forward to getting to Cape Coast Castle as we shall get such a lot of letters or papers. I hope that I shall get all the letters that you are sending to the Cape to me.

I have just turned out the contents of my ditty box and I find I have such a lot of nice things. I'm going to send my watch home in the box because I want you please to get it mended and cleaned for me. I want one very badly but because I have as aide-de-camp to take the times of the evolutions and I don't like borrowing the Captain's or First Lieutenant's gold watches because I always fear that one of these days I shall smash them. I am looking forward to getting the photo of Heppington soon. I'm making such a splendid plan of the house, one storey high (old-fashioned) I will send you a copy when done. It requires a lot of Head[ache] to do it though, I can tell you. I am making such a splendid horsey scrapbook. I want you to hang the picture up somewhere in my room, it is a duplicate of the one on the little page in my book. I assure you the book will be very amusing. There are also a lot of newspaper cuttings in it, so I want you to send any more old newspaper cuttings about us or anybody else so that I can put them in my book. I have just been reading Shakespeare's *Richard II* so am of course greatly edified. It is beginning to be awfully hot, I hate the heat so. I don't know what to say more, so goodbye darlings all.

HMS *Dido*, June 11, 1880 St Helena

We are back again at St Helena, not much of a place after the Cape. I had enough money to have a ride, so I had one, a good one too, but as it is rather amusing and as I had a couple of croppers, though happily I did not hurt myself, I will begin the yarn properly and end up properly.

On the 10th, yesterday, the second day after our arrival in here, I went ashore with Bruce (one of the mids) and we got a couple of horses – mine was "Percy" and his "Nimrod". Nimrod was the biggest horse, [so] as Bruce was the biggest he had him. Well, I wore my tight riding breeches which Lindsay gave me and we mounted the beasts in the middle of the road under some trees and as my horse had not been ridden for some time, there being no ship in here, he was awfully fresh and was kicking and rearing like anything, and once he got his hindquarters inside the door of a cottage and I thought I was coming off but I did not. Then

Signal flags flown at St Helena Signal Station by B. G-F

I thrashed him as hard as I could and at last he stopped for a second and then away he tore as hard as beans across a small brook and did not stop until we got to the foot of some of these enormous hills which are in the place. Well, we rode on up winding paths generally, going off the proper road because we wanted to see as much of the beautiful scenery as was possible, and in one place it was beautiful – we were just at the bottom of a valley and we could see two waterfalls about 50 feet tall just in front of us, and heaps of wild red geraniums and thousands of those large cactuses and another small kind of tropical tree that only blossoms once in several years (it is in blossom now) in abundance. It was the most beautiful view I ever saw, I think; the cliffs are higher, though not quite as precipitous in places as the Cheddar Cliffs.

Well, we got to the top soon and we galloped along and I generally managed to get ahead of Bruce although his horse was considered the best of the two. Well, nothing of interest occurred for another quarter mile until we came to a long level part, though with two very sharp corners in it. So we got equal and started at full gallop and tore round this corner, endangering the life of any unfortunate individuals who might have happened to be near, because the horses pulled most awfully and nothing will stop them suddenly when they are in full gallop, like we went. Well, in the midst of it, I was ahead and Bruce was drawing gradually ahead so I gave my horse the reins and whip and we flew. Bruce's cap came off but we could not stop. On! On! On! we tore. Now you must know that about 500 yards further on there was a small path turning off from the main road, just wide enough for two horses uncomfortably abreast of one another. Well, the path leads down a pretty steep hill towards Napoleon's tomb, and the horses are unfortunately used to going down this path but as we had already seen Napoleon's tomb we did not care to go down, so tore on, when suddenly our horses turned down the steep path at full gallop – and to our horror we saw the wooden gate in front of us about halfway down the hill, *shut*. It was much too high for them to jump, especially as we were going so fast and downhill, so we tugged and tugged but it was worse in my case. Bruce's horse gradually came to an anchor before we reached the gate but mine did not decrease his speed till we were about 4 yards off when he suddenly stopped and I found myself on my seat of honour in the mud about 2 yards in front of my horse, having gone clean over his head – but, I thank goodness, mud is soft so I was not hurt. I had kept hold of his reins, so he did not run away. So I remounted and quietly got onto the main road and we went back and found Bruce's cap. And now Chapter 1 being finished I must have my 9:00 pm cup of cocoa.

I have just had it (Anglo-Swiss Cocoa and Milk (preserved)). Well then, we went on about 1½ miles further to a place called Huts Gate, 1780 feet above the level of the sea and ordered our tea to be ready for us in half an hour's time. Six poached eggs and ham (same as you, Papa, and myself had in Monmouth when we were fishing), [and] any amount of tea, bread and butter, and in the meantime we rode out towards Longwood and much the same thing happened over again. We were galloping harder than before when suddenly rounding a corner we saw a five barred iron gate shut, so my horse did just the same as last time but I went further over his head this time than before and hurt my side a little, too. It is all right now. I could not help laughing though. Well, I remounted and went through and got onto some level place behind Longwood House and there we had some good gallops and I tried to make my beast jump the ditch but he would not, so we came back and had our own good tea (and now the mid of this watch wants me to relieve him while he gets some tea) so good night for the present.

June 13, 1880

After our tea we rode quietly down to the town when we came on board, the time being about 6:30 pm. I have not been ashore since this very enjoyable day. The *Humber* came here from Cape way, and brought me two such delicious [letters] and the books. I hope you address all my letters to the West Coast. Thank you so *frightfully awfully much* for the most superb and *delicious* book called "Sketches in the Hunting Field". I'm so thankful to you for it.

Mr Nicholls said the other day I was working very well at study and heard him tell the captain, so that is good news is it not? And now I will answer your letters. From the letter of May 6, 1880 – I am so glad my letter about my leave was agreeable to you. I hope I shall soon be able to write as agreeable a one!!! Excuse my bad writing but the mail is going soon. It was very kind of Major Parr to write kindly about me. I think, yes, I have received two parcels. I send you a little scribble which I drew entirely from my head. I want you to keep them so that you can see if I improve at all. Remember me to Nurse, I'm glad you like the seeds.

June 14, midnight

I'm so glad Papa is going to be raised a step tonight with the Free Masons. I'm so very glad that Dico is going to spend a week in London, only I don't expect he will see so much or enjoy himself half so much during his week as I enjoyed my darling and ever to be remembered week with Granny and the Aunts.

Now for your letter and Nora's and darling little May Bees of May 13, 1880. I am so much obliged to dear little baby for her charming letter. I'm so glad Mr Michaelson wrote a good account of me. It was very good of him and I'm so glad he is feeling better. I'm so glad you, mother, got such a lot of nice birthday presents. I only wish I had been able to send you one. I must wish you *very many happy returns* of the day though it is very late to do so – but the saying is "better late than never". Please remember me kindly to Carry Walwyn and Miss Hartland. It was very lucky that the book and your letter which came in the *American* was sewed.[21] Nora says that you, Papa, have bought such a nice new cabinet for the dining room. I want you to please send me about half a dozen of the big plates you put in the beginning of books with our arms and crests on it. You know what I mean. I want to put one in my new book and don't want you to crop my name, Papa, at the bottom of them.

A French line of battle ship came in here the other day, she is used for taking prisoners to and from New Caledonia Island. She has got about 18 communists on board that she is taking back to France, their time of imprisonment having expired. She is frightfully dirty, I believe. I have not been on-board her yet. All today (Sunday) they were playing a barrel organ and dancing on the Quarterdeck. I really don't know of anything more to say. I believe we go out of this place next Wednesday. Tomorrow, Monday, we are giving a dance on board but I don't think I shall put in an appearance as I shall be very tired indeed because I have been on deck the whole of today. And now I really am stumped as to what more to say – I did not send the box of curios by the *Humber* as she only waited here a few hours and there was not time to have the box made, but they will easily keep and send some other time.

And now, darlings at home, darlings at Rockenham all, good night and good bye for the present. Kisses ad libitum.

From your loving son

Brian G Godfrey Faussett

HMS *Dido* at sea, June 19, 1880

We have left nice St Helena and are on our way to Ascension, which you know I have not seen before. We're only going to stay there a few days. I'm halfway through "Sketches in the Hunting Field". I have lent it to one of our horsey lieutenants who is greatly pleased with it. We gave a dance on board the other day, it was not a great success though it was fun – after the dance I went with our chaplain to have tea with a Lady Ross (I did not dance at all during the dance because I was on duty for the whole time). Well, we arrived rather late for tea but we had a good tea nevertheless and afterwards I was asked to go to

---

21 perhaps sewn into a parcel of oilcloth for safekeeping on board

a house in the same grounds … We danced away and had great fun till 1230. When we came on board I'm sorry to say that I had to turn out at 4 o'clock to keep the morning watch.

We expect to be back at St Helena by October. We have made a very good passage that time going under sail alone 10 or 11 kn. We have been having a lot of French officers on board from the big line of battle ship *Jago* (?) that was at St Helena, and we were jabbering away in French like anything. It is getting awfully hot. I'm afraid I must stop now as I have got to go on deck to take the altitude of the moon to find our longitude by. We expect to get into Ascension by 4 pm tomorrow (Sunday) I'm going to write a letter to Lindsay tomorrow. Good night darlings, English and Irish all.

June 20, 1880. Sunday

We are in sight of Ascension –… I must wait till I have seen the place before I go spinning all these yarns –

June 23

Lots of news to tell you next time, but the mail is just going without any warning. I had a walk of about 20 miles yesterday onto the top of a mountain 2802 feet high.

Ascension Island, June 26, 1880

We are off to sea this evening for Cape Coast Castle, when we will get all our papers. We are going to leave our mail behind here and I believe the letters we leave get home five days before those we send at Cape Coast Castle. We will have a passage of 10 or 12 days to Cape C C.

I had such fun the other day. Mr Ashworth asked me to walk up to the top of Green Mountain with him. It is a little over a mile away and it is 2800 feet above the level of the sea. So we started at 6:30pm on Thursday in our strongest boots and with big sticks, and walked up to the foot of the mountain about 3½ miles and then by George we began the ascent and it was an ascent with a vengeance – there were two or three tanks on the way so we had a drink now and then but it was awful and I nearly died!!! But at last we got to the top and we found that the Marine who used to keep a refreshment house had gone to England, so we were in the greatest state of agony but we were led to the house of the farmer bailiff, the man who does all the farming on the island

and supplies the ships with flesh, beef, mutton et cetera, so we sat down as
he was not finished dressing. By the time he was dressed and came out I had
got my wind back again so he took us into his little room and we talked about
everything, crops cattle et cetera and we discovered that he had been educated
at Magdalen College Oxford, so we were very happy that we had fallen in
with such a nice gentleman. So then he proposed that we should walk round
his garden (but before I go any further I ought to tell you how long we took to
get up. We took a little under two hours, not bad was it?) – So we said yes and
he took us round his garden, such a nice garden, flowers as well as vegetables.
It is just like England, and he took us over to his lawn tennis ground.

We discovered that he was awfully fond of lawn tennis so we said we
would have some games at about 12 o'clock and as it was an awfully good
ground, clay and a full-size and wire all round to keep the balls from going we
looked forward to it with some joy; but then he thought that breakfast must
be ready so we went back and as it was not quite ready we waited outside the
house humbugging his dogs. He has got a lot of dogs; one splendid retriever
that will do next to anything. He says he has never lost a ball yet because the
dog always brings them to him. He threw some balls as far as he could into a
lot of bushes and trees and the dog went in and after looking for a short time
for them brought them all back. We had taken our own little terrier Scamp
up with us so we were sitting down when we suddenly saw a frightened hen
rushing round the corner of the house with Scamp after her, so we chased
them. Finally the dog caught the hen in a small hole in the rock and we also
caught the dog so we gave him a very good flogging.

Fortunately the hen was not hurt so then then we went back and found
that breakfast was ready, so in we went and found a most delicious repast
of poached eggs and bacon, so we made an enormous meal, and then Mr
Spearman (the farmer) proposed that we should go around the farm with him
as he was going his morning rounds so we went and saw all his cattle and
horses; lots of things, all very interesting indeed. Then he left us on top of a
hill to go to sleep and read while he went round the fields. Mr Ashworth had
a *London Society* and I had a couple of *Fields*, so we buried ourselves in our
own papers and Mr Ashworth gave me a cheroot to smoke. Soon the farmer
came back to us so we went down again, just stopping at the farm to look at
a brood of young ducks that had lately come out of their shells, and met two
of our mids, Tawney and Williams, on their way up; then we sat in the house
again and jawed, and soon our chaplain, Mr Nicholls, and Mr Heyward, our
Navigating Lieutenant, appeared at the door. So in they came and had a drink,
and then we all sallied forth to the tennis ground where we had some splendid

games. I liked it awfully; we played for more than one hour, then we came back to a splendid lunch, duck and fowls. In the midst of which our Captain appeared, riding uphill on a grey horse, the property of Captain Rowe, the Captain of the island, so he came in and had little lunch. Then we went out, looked at the stables and then went through a long tunnel of ¼ of a mile long and only just room for one to walk, and pitch dark. It led from Mr Spearman's gardens to a valley called Black Meadow Valley, a very pretty place.

From there Mr Nicholls and Mr Heyward went down again to go on board as it was getting rather late in the day. The Captain and myself went and played some more tennis and had tea then we started down again, the captain on his horse and us two walking so of course we soon left the captain behind. We tried to make some shortcuts but lost our way and nearly broke our necks on the sandstone. The ground is simply awful, you can imagine that a lot of hard lava is, simply awful for walking on and it was quite dark (I'm writing the most awful nonsense am I not!) Well we got on board at last at 8 o'clock and I dined with the Captain and I turned in much the worse for wear. I ought to tell you that nobody lives on this island except people employed by the service. I don't suppose anybody would live there if they had the chance because there is no cultivation at all except on Green Mountain.

The next day there was a cricket match between us and the island, and we beat them all to nothing. There is a great huge saltwater lake on shore, 100′ × 25′, and I had a beautiful cold bathe. I bought some delicious chocolate creams which I enjoyed thoroughly.

Yesterday I walked out to a place called Wide Awake Farm with Tawney and Miles and saw a sight worth seeing. Thousands of these birds flying about and laying eggs all over the place. I had to shove a bird off her eggs sometimes to get one. We brought back a few eggs and ate them on the ship. They were very nice but there were not many eggs as the Marines and the stewards had been there just before to get a lot of eggs for the garrison, they are simply wonderfully tame. I knocked several down with my stick just hitting about over my head but of course I did not kill any because you are not to kill them. They all try to attack you but they dare not. We walked back after we had satisfied our curiosity and I was really awfully tired. Nothing has happened since then which was yesterday. There is to be a return match played today. And now my darlings I must say goodbye until I get to that horrible place called Cape Coast Castle – love and kisses to all the darlings in Ireland and elsewhere …

Cape Coast Castle, July 10, 1880

We had a very fine passage from Ascension, it took 11 days, and now we are
melting away on the West Coast again. I am going onshore this afternoon with
Williams although there is nothing to do when you get there. On the way here
we bathed overboard three times. I dived off the nettings (top of the bulwarks
to me – an old expression) a good height, you know. We were in dread of
being eaten by sharks the whole time, but there is very little chance of that
when there are so many bathing, because any of the ships company that cared
to did, so although, of course, we kept away from them … The examination is
going to begin on Monday next the 12th …

July 16, 1880

– I went onshore yesterday afternoon but did nothing much. It was awfully
hot, and we went round to see the goldsmiths shop and watched them making
jewellery, some of which was very pretty and made out of gold only, made
by the natives sitting down in these horrible houses nearly naked – so stuffy.
I did not come off shore completely empty handed, though, so you may be
sure you may expect something soon. I cannot send it yet as there is no chance
of anybody going home. Whilst we were in one place, another native came
rushing with some gold dust about £5 worth which had just been brought from
the country, and they both were awfully delighted about it. We also went and
looked at the lighthouse on the hill, and now it is really too hot to write any
more. I am perspiring in a manner horrible – Love to all the Irish and English
ones.

Off Brass River, August 2, 1880

There is going to be a bit of a row here sometime soon I believe. The captain
has been up the river twice in the gunboat *Decoy,* holding palavers with the
natives, and if they do not give up a certain fine – 300 puncheons of palm oil
– before a certain date, we are going to blockade the river or something of the
sort. You may see something about it in the papers …

Have you seen that article in the 'United Service Gazette' about the new
Report that has to be made on all officers half yearly? There has been an awful
lot of rows about it and I expect that it will get knocked on the head altogether,
because, of course, it is an awfully foolish thing.

I believe I have grown tremendously since you last saw me and I am getting a charming moustache!!! The Consul came with us from Fernando Po because he is doing his business up the River Brass with the Captain. His name is Hewit, a brother of Admiral Hewit who was Commodore on this station for so long.

We are anchored about 4 miles off the shore and rolling piteously, and now adieu because it is high time that I had my 3 cups (large) of cocoa – I've been bribing the Cook by a bottle of beer to make me a cake for tea … In the gun room we have been living on little else but salt pork and salt horse, or beef as you would call it, so I am naturally getting thinner. Besides that all we have to eat is that hard biscuit all day instead of bread, except at breakfast when we get a lump of dough each. These lumps of dough they call rolls so you can imagine that your "Dainty Cockle" does not eat much.

Captain Domvile has just gone ashore. He is to spend the night with the governor or some such personage. You have to go to the shore a distance of 7 miles in a steamer which crosses the bar, one of the greatest in the world and swarming with horrible sharks!' Shudder, I do. I went ashore last time we were here just for the sake of saying that I had been across the bar; you cannot cross it in a small boat. It is the rainy season here and all about this part of the coast, which is not pleasant as it ruins your gear et cetera. And now, darlings all, goodbye love and kisses to all Irish ones.

HMS *Dido*, Accra, August 15, 1880

We have been rolling heavily all today, 13° both ways sometimes, and this morning during divine service the forms that the men sit on collapsed; and some of the officers chairs, mine included, also got fidgety, so that it was quite laughable especially for the *Midshipmen* … Yesterday afternoon I saw a very pretty sight: there were about 38 small canoes with their large single white sail set, sailing towards the ship – it looks very pretty. They go out at night – with six natives in each to fish and come in next day and sell the fish. The natives here live almost entirely on fish, yams and bananas. I do not care about yams, but if they are good they make a very good substitute for potato.

The other day the Captain took me out shooting with him. We took a krooman with us to carry our game and cartridges and we walked altogether about 12 miles. I was simply dead tired. Our bag when we came on board consisted of a brace of turkey buzzards, he shot one and I the other. They are beautiful large birds (we are not going to eat now for one or two days?); we had crossed the pond and were walking through the long grass up to our waist when the bird rose about 30 feet in front of me and flew away from me so I raised my shotgun and shot him with *my* gun. The captain fired both his barrels at one just before me and missed, [but] he shot his bird nearer the end of the day. I'm having the wing of mine preserved. I also fired and missed a partridge, and I also fired and killed another large uneatable bird on the wing. The Captain shot a partridge which he could not find in the long grass, and he shot at a small buck but as he had number four shot in his gun instead of buckshot he failed to kill it. When we were coming back I was so dead tired I could hardly walk, so while the captain was being carried across the ford by the krooman I spread his waterproof out, lay down on it and actually went to sleep – a very foolish thing to do. Then the krooman woke me up and carried me across; we got on board about 8:30 pm and I turned in, dead tired. Love to all darlings.

HMS *Dido*, From Accra/Cape Coast Castle, August 25, 1880, Thursday night

I forgot to tell you in my last letter that when I was out shooting with the Captain we saw a young Cobra (snake) and shot and wounded him; he curled round the muzzle of my gun because I was not aware of the fact of his being poisonous though he soon got knocked off when the Captain told me about the poison … The Captain is going to give me a wing of his turkey buzzard as mine is rather knocked about, but I have kept mine.

The other day I went ashore at Accra with one of our assistant Clerks who has just passed for Clerk, and I took my little money ashore in mother's purse and bought besides two reels of cotton, three skins, one of a long-haired big black monkey or gorilla, another of a different but very beautiful monkey, and last, but by no means least, a long well marked skin of a large gold bush cat, just like a leopard only not so large. I shall send them home when an opportunity arises with the other curiosities I have collected. I'm going to, if I can get a good one, buy a native chair or stool, they are very nice and curiously carved. The men here are the most indecent of any we have encountered yet. Some of them men go about entirely without a scrap of clothing on and the women very little. The evening we came off there was a very bad surf, and when we got into the surf boat all the natives who had dry clothing on took them off and we got through the surf safely, I'm naturally glad to say. Enormous waves break but the light surf boat gets over them all safely.

August 28, Saturday, Cape Coast Castle

Yesterday we had played single sticks on the quarterdeck and some of us fenced a little. This afternoon just as I was going off to a nice sleep the Captain sent for me and asked me if I would like to go ashore with him, so, of course, I had to say yes and he said he would take another mid – we did not do much onshore because there was nothing much to be done, and there was no excitement getting through the surf because there was very little surf. He went into a black goldsmiths shop because he wanted to see about buying a bracelet made for Miss Mary Frere as she had asked him to get some coast jewellery for her to the value of £5. We learnt a few things from the captain during the walk, one of which was that we are going sometime soon to a place called Cape Lopez, near here I believe, where there are any amount of buffaloes, and he says he believes they come down to the waters. If so, I bet I have a shot at one; very nice if I could keep the skin and horns of a beast I shot myself! I should have to take a ship's rifle of course, and I believe you have to stay ashore all night. We also learnt that there was very little chance of us going down to the Cape for a very long while.

On shore I saw a native girl with her hair done up with eight spikes, each about 3 inches long, but there are creatures going about with hair done up more curiously than that, only I cannot remember them. We saw a girl, evidently some native swell, going about the town shaking hands with everyone, she wore nothing but a long silk cloth coming up to her waist and her hair, which was funnily dressed, was all covered with native gold ornaments. I should think she carried over a hundred pounds worth of gold ornaments on her head.

The most frightful heavy dew falls every night – very hard for the mids keeping the night watch – and now I must say good night as I am at a loss for something to say. I enclose a piece of verse that I made up myself about my not getting my boots.

My Boots
The Mail is coming in today,
Tomorrow we will all get our pay
So both combined, I have no doubt
Will make us all both laugh and shout
If my box of boots don't come I'll swear
Because at present I've nothing to wear
I also hope some letters there will be
Especially, that is to say, for me

(The day after, mail has not come in)

> The mail is not come in, oh horror!
> For having no boots you know is a bother
> I think I had better go on the sick list
> With a broken toe or a sprained wrist
> Then at Divisions I won't have to be,
> And the Captain can't laugh at me, no not he.

Compiled and sung by B G Godfrey-Faussett.
First day of Partridge Shooting 1880

HMS *Dido*, Jellacoffee, September 20, 1880

I cannot write much of a letter this time so I shall write to granny, because I'm very tired, having been on deck walking up and down the whole day … There was a grand excitement on deck. We saw about 3 porpoises a mile distant and a swordfish fighting with a whale. It was very amusing, the enormous splashing and big bodies appearing above the surface of the water every now and then. There are lots of whales round this part of the coast. We have been coaling ship all day and it is a very dirty piece of work I can tell you, so if this letter is not as clean as it might be you will excuse it on account of the coal dust that is flying about. We are only taking on 80 tons which is a good thing. The other day we all went out sailing in one of the cutters and had great fun. Monckton brought his lines and rod and some minnows. We caught one fine mackerel and we presented it to the captain. Our steward has just come to ask us for 9 black silk handkerchieves, worth about 14 shillings altogether, to give to a native for seven fine big turkeys. The Captain inspected HMS *Fram* today. No sign of my poor boots yet.

HMS *Dido*, off Brass River, September 28, 1880

There is very little news. The Captain went up the river yesterday in the gunboat *Firebrand*, and found that the fine had been paid, so I'm sorry to say there will be no row at all. We have great fun now after evening Quarters skylarking and humbugging about. I had a single stick fight the other day with Black, each of us riding on the shoulder of a big fellow. It was great fun and I think I went I went to windward. I got another crack on the top of the skull but it did not hurt too much …

HMS *Dido*, Fernando Po, October 8, 1880

I am afraid you will not get letters quite so regularly now as we are going down the coast and therefore miss the steamers sometimes. I missed writing a letter by the last mail but there was nothing to say. We are at this beautiful place once more. The other day I went out shooting with Monckton, Williams and Nicholson. We did not have much sport and it was very wet. I'm going to try to go out shooting tomorrow by myself if no one will come with me. I'm going to try and get a few pigeons as they say there are some on the island …

After we leave this place it is my turn to begin my three month keeping Officer of the Watch. I have to relieve the deck at 8 o'clock in the morning (at sea) till 8.30, and keep the 4 to 8 in the evening every day, so I shall have to keep my eyes open to prevent an *Atalanta* case, and I shall also have to carry on if any sails are to be set or anything done – of course the Captain will always be up if there's anything much to be done. I shall have to yell like anything. I don't mind though, because it is an awfully good thing for me. The captain asked Tawney and myself to dine with him the other night when we were at sea and help him to eat his Michaelmas goose so we were both dressed and up in his cabin waiting for him to come up when suddenly the awful cry of "Man overboard" was heard so we rushed out and I dug out at getting the lifeboat lowered et cetera. The Captain was on deck in an instant and the ship was very soon "hove to"; she was under all plain sail at the time, going at about 3 knots. The lifebuoy of course was let go at first and the light on it burned beautifully, so after a little excitement it was discovered the wretched man was hanging on to a rope which he had collared as he fell, so we soon picked him up and got the lifebuoy in and proceeded on our way. We discovered that the wretched man, whose name was Freeman, could not swim so it was lucky he had hold of the rope or he would probably have been drowned. That's all about that, but the yell "man overboard" sounded very ghastly to me. It was the first and I hope the last [time] I ever hear it; it was pitch dark at the time.

Well, after all it was happy, the Captain and we continued our dinner in the middle of which another rather funny[22] thing happened; the doctor came up and announced that a Krooman who had been sick for some time had just died, so we went on shore next day to bury him. So that was a very ghastly evening was it not?

There is an awful row going on … I'm afraid that you will find some greasy spots on this paper as drops of perspiration are continuing continually

---

22 Used in the sense of 'weird/unusual/noteworthy'

falling off my forehead!!! We are going to Cape Lopez where all the buffaloes
and wild pigs are. I hope to have some sport there … The cockroaches are
getting horribly numerous in the gun room. I slaughter them whenever I get a
chance. The rats are also awfully numerous but not in the gun room!!! It is my
middle watch tonight and I'm sure I don't know how I shall keep it because I
am awfully tired. I had a huge dose of quinine too, the evening after I had been
onshore. I did not like it at all. The doctor has left off giving it to us in sherry
because he found out, I suppose, it was too expensive!! I hope everybody is
well and happy at the several homes. I wish I was with you darlings. Now I
must bid you goodbye, love to darling granny and others. I'm quite well and
all that kind of thing – my tooth aches now and then, that's all.

HMS *Dido*, Accra, November 19th 1880

I believe this letter will arrive home Just about Xmas time, so I wish you all
a very Merry Xmas; 'all' includes everybody in Ireland as well as at home.
Thanks, Mary, for your letter. You will have received by now a small note
from the last mail. I hope dear old 'Fermor' is getting well and strong again.
You seem to have been gadding about in December … I think I'll copy what I
can out of my diary:-

At Fernando Po October 9th

I showed my log and new chart to the Captain and asked leave to go on
shore shooting, he gave me leave and was very nice … At 2 pm I went
on shore with Bruce, taking guns and heaps of cartridges. Bruce took
William's gun and we both expected to shoot lots of pigeons. A short
way up the avenue I took a wild path leading inland and succeeded in
losing my way and seeing no pigeons. I met lots of very curious boobies
(natives), some naked with long hair and very savage looking. I heard
Bruce firing twice, and so I sat down greatly disappointed and then
began to find my way and chased a pigeon which had flown across and
which Bruce saw emerging from some bushes and fired at but missed.

We met Mr Nicholls, then after that we went to the big beastly Spanish
House in the middle of the Avenue, where we drank some foul water
and had a ripe pineapple. We saw that horrible looking white native boy,
he is exactly like a native in every way except that he has a yellow white
colour and he has a squint. I forgot to say that soon after I left Bruce I

was walking in the thickest part of the bush, making my way towards a grove of trees, when I saw a small black monkey with a long tail in one of the trees, so I changed my cartridge, which was a five, for a buckshot cartridge – but by the time I had shifted the monkey had disappeared.

Well, after we left the Spanish House we came down to Holt's where we drank a bottle of not good beer and a tin of biscuits. Then we came down to the boat, meeting the Spanish Governor on the way. When we got on board I had some quinine, and after dinner I turned in, much the worse for wear. I forgot to say that in the course of our walking onshore we met a native who had shot five jolly little porcupines, just the same size of a small pig. He gave me some of the quills.

Fernando Po October 10 Sunday

My morning watch, plenty of work and slanging from Number One (the First Lieutenant, Lt. Prickett). Mail came in and brought us lots of letters. Had a splendid sleep in the afternoon.

Fernando Po October 11 Monday

Got underway at about 4 pm. Went on deck and began keeping my office of the watch for the first time. There was no sail set so I did not mind much. We were steaming, going about 5 knots. The Captain was in very good humour.

From Fernando Po to Batango Tuesday, October 12

Relieved Mr Bland. 6 am Heyward sent me down to shift into Blues[23] as it was coming on to rain, so when I relieved him it came down in torrents. Did nothing much during the day. The midshipmen all went to seamanship with the Boatswain in the afternoon. We got into Batango anchorage in the forenoon. Lots of trees at Batango, a beautiful waterfall by the beach and two houses. The Captain landed and had a native spear given to him, and some of the wardroom officers went off sailing in the gig. Batango was the place where the Commodore had done all the fighting with the natives.

October 12 Monday Fernando Po

I forgot all about the 100lb torpedo fired at this place. The Spanish

---

23 Blue uniform for colder climes (as against whites for tropical)

Governor came off to see it. It was placed by divers in the middle of a wreck and when it was fired it blew very little of the wreck above water and killed very few fish. Monckton, Garforth, Bruce, Nicholson and myself [were] sent away in the gig, taking a blue jacket with us, and we picked up a few fish which were good eating.

October 13, Wednesday, from Batango to River Gabon.

Got underway at 5:30 am, I relieved the deck at 6:15 am. Very fine at first but from 7 to 8.30 it rained in torrents. I got wet through although it did not blow much and we were under fore and aft sail doing 5 knots. Came down below at 8.30 for my breakfast tired and wet through. Went to school in forenoon; it rained on and off the whole forenoon. Took sights at noon and kept the dog watches.

From Batango to R. Gabon October 14.

I turned out to relieve the deck at 5.30 very tired. The Captain gave me some of his bananas.

From Batango to R. Gabon October 15

Got wet through in the morning watch. Wet all day. Got into Gabon, at anchor about 1.5 miles from the town Libreville. Found it quite a busy place compared to the wretched places on the coast. It is a French port, and ivory is the principal export. In the afternoon we saluted the French Flag with 21 guns and we afterwards heard that the French returned the salute but we could not hear or see it as they only had rotten little brass guns. In the evening Captain Domvile and Captain Sisson (*Firebrand*) went to call on the French governor, in cocked hats, epaulettes and swords, and Monckton went in the same gig to call on the French officers on board the big hulk but he did not see anybody. He came on board saying he was very glad because he said he did not want to show off his French before them.

In Gabon R. Oct. 16th, Saturday

H E the French Governor and the suite came on board this morning. Received them with a guard of honour. At 2 o'clock Number One sent all the mids on board a French barque to see how they got a huge 15 ton cutter out. Garforth and Nicholson, who had gone ashore shooting, came on board in the evening with a brace of pigeons both of which I think fell to Garforth's gun.

R. Gabon October 18 Monday.

Heavy rain all the forenoon. The acting French Governor or came on board to lunch with the Captain, and afterwards H.E. and suite came round the lower deck and examined the gun room. Got underway at 3 pm and started for Cape Lopez. Kept the two dog watches, during which time Hayward was showing me how to navigate the ship out of the river. Captain in very good humour. Rained the last dog watch.

Cape Lopez October 19

We arrived at this place at 11 o'clock and anchored about 500 yards offshore in about 25 fathoms. We were anchored in Cape Lopez Bay and the shore looked very pretty not hilly, but perfectly flat. Captain Domvile, Vickers and nearly all the *Firebrand* officers shot three between them. Capt D and Mr V shot more. The Captain would shoot at them at 500 yards so of course could not kill them.

Cape Lopez 20th.

The Port watch went ashore swimming and caught a fine fish. Crawford was the only officer with them. Nicholson, Monckton, Williams, Bruce, Nicholls, Barry and self all started from the ship at 7.30, each armed with a rifle and about 30 rounds of ammunition, taking two Kroomen and John Pitt, servant, and lots of freshwater and grub with us.

Well, we all landed in the gig and started to walk out to a place where we might pitch our camp. We found a convenient spot about 2 ½ miles from where we landed and there we left our provisions and two of the Firebrand's Kroomen. Two of ditto have come ashore to bring back the heads of the animals that have been shot the day before. Then we walked on having loaded our rifles and after some time one of the Kroomen sighted a buffalo grazing by himself in the middle of a place so we became quiet, then immediately put our pipes out, and after some more looking we discovered 30 more near the bushes. They were about 150 yards off so we divided into two parties, Monckton, Bruce, Nicholson, and Williams and the Kroomen going to the right, Mr

Nicholls, Barry, myself and John Pitt going off to the left.

We both got behind the bushes on opposite sides and walked quickly and carefully along, when suddenly from out of the bushes walked another herd of about 40 buffalo. We immediately laid down and sighted our rifles for 300 yards, then we saw them beginning to run away so we each fired a shot but they had no effect, being too far of course. There was no use going after these any more because once startled they will go on for about 5 miles or more before they stop and graze. Well, we walked on and on trying to get a shot for about 1 mile when suddenly on the other side of the bush on our right we heard shot after shot fired, about 25 altogether; they were the other party firing at the buffalo we had first seen.

Well, we went on and on trying to get a shot at the buffaloes which were such a long way off from us. We went on about 7 miles and then we had a shock as Barry left us. But then just as we were walking on, a small herd of about 20 appeared walking through the bush so we got behind the bushes and ran after them as hard as we could, scratching our hands and faces with thorns but when we got to the end of the bushes, behold they were about 300 yards distant in the plain and they were all walking quickly on, but we followed them for about 3 miles further. Then we got into a thicket in the middle of the prairie and our small herd met a large herd and then they all began eating away in the grass at about 600 yards from us- there were about 200. Old Nichols had taken his boots off a long time before and had forgotten to say. Wretched John Pitt had to carry them for him. Well, we all lay down *frightfully tired*. With our rifles loaded and alongside of us we had a good sleep of about one hour, only the sun which was rather hot and the trees did not shade us much, so we had to make awnings out of our handkerchiefs.

Well then, we got up and shook ourselves. I could hardly shake myself I was so tired! Then we saw the herd where we had seen them before we went to sleep, so Nicholls and I loaded our rifles and we crawled along for about quarter of a mile on our hands and knees through burnt grass, burnt by the sun. So as I got to the opposite side and to leeward of the beasts we saw that there were five of them by themselves, some little way from the others, so we thought we might try and get a couple of them, so we crawled along, and when we were about 200 yards off old Nicholls got tired of crawling along so he stood up and said we would fire, so we each fired a shot. I fired first, and we each hit our beast and they promptly looked round for a second before rushing away to our right. We thought at first they were going to charge us and the remainder of the herd galloped away from us, so we quickly loaded again and I picked the last one and we both fired about three shots each. I hit my beast and wounded him, as did Nicholls his, but they crawled and limped into the jungle. We were running after them but they got into the jungle just too soon so we lost our wounded animals; so, awfully tired and horribly disappointed, we began to wend our *weary, weary* way back.

After about quarter mile walking or rather dragging, we sighted three huts so we made for them hoping to get some native who for a little dash[24] could carry our gear, but when we got there we found they were empty, But instead we found two delicious deep pools of cold water amongst the trees, so I wet myself all over and drank about three tons of water from the other, filled my little bottle and then on we trudged again. But it would be too long if I were to give it all in detail, it is enough to say that we came across tracks of wild boar and deer and we drank tons of hot water out of every out of every pool we saw and I did get back somehow. Old Nichols allowed me then to lie down and sleep for five minutes but when we came in sight of the first of our fellows, Williams and Bruce, they took my rifle from me and I fell down and could hardly move, so Williams carried my rifle for me and Bruce helped me, and *somehow* I got back to the camp one and three-quarter miles further on. The fellows informed me they thought I was going to die I looked so utterly miserable and done up – and so by Jove I was. I was never half so tired in my life before and I sincerely hope and trust I shall never be half so tired again.

The other fellows there told me that they had shot three buffaloes, Williams 2, Monckton 1 and Bruce and Nicholson 1 between them, so

---

24 money

we were very unfortunate having done all the work and got none of the fun. When we got to the camp I lay down in Monckton's waterproof sheet, drank cocoa which Bruce made for me, and a glass of beer and potted meat and biscuits again and stuffed myself and then, leaning on Bruce's arm, I got down to the boat. It was pitch dark now of course so that we were continually falling over mounds and other things. We fired a rifle off on the beach to attract attention and the gig came in and we went on board and had some supper at 9 pm and turned in *very, very, very* much the worse for buffalo hunting. We, the midshipmen, were comforted with the news that we were excused our night watches for that night.

October 21 Cape Lopez.

We all went out surveying at 0830. My bones were all sticking out of my body in all directions and I was lame and stiff. We got on board again just before lunch. In the afternoon I went ashore with the swimming party, Nicholls, Miller and myself in the pinnace with all the men, taking with us some sweet biscuits and potted cocoa; we did not catch many fish, one big salmon. We got about 100 fish altogether! Coming off in the pinnace we had some songs from the men.

October 22nd

Kept the forenoon watch. I got leave to go ashore with the swimming party again for a wander, but first of all I started at 3 o'clock with my gun with 12 cartridges in the cutter to go ashore and see if I could shoot anything. Williams also came with his gun and I shot a sand piper out of the cutter, which I gave to a blue jacket. When we got on shore we separated. I made for a clump of trees which I saw in the distance, and Williams went along the shore. I heard him firing lots of shots and I shot a couple of very fine plump pigeons. They were awfully wild and they were very difficult to get out after I had shot them because of the thick bush into which they fell. I winged another but could not get him and another fell dead into the midst of a thorny bush.

About 5 o'clock I came back with my game and found that Williams had only shot a couple of sand snipe. I also found the swimming party ashore all running about in bathing drawers, making a huge fire. I found that Miller and Barry had come ashore with them, and Miller and John Pitt were in the act of making some cocoa which was very welcome to me. I gave the bluejackets a couple of pots of cocoa which they liked very much, then I took my boots and socks off and lent my gun to Barry who did not shoot anything, and then I helped to haul the canoe and got wet through in the twinkling of an eye: it soon got very dark and so nearly all the blue jackets were near the fire cooking the fish. Monckton, Miller, Barry and self and a chosen few, about 12, blue jackets made a fire about ¼ mile away from the other and hauled the seine[25] about six times and got over 100 fish, all fine mullet, and then had to stop because our recall had been up about two hours; so we all got into the pinnace and came on board in the middle of songs and it was the happiest day I had spent for a long time, shooting and swimming combined.

October 23rd Cape Lopez, Saturday.

Captain Domvile, Mr Ogle, Mr Ashworth, Mr Nicholls, Mr Ayling and Mr Roots, Monckton, Bruce and Nicholson all started early in the morning to go out for a long day's buffalo shooting taking some Kroomen with them. I had to stay on board as it was my day on, and the first lieutenant was also on board. Well, I kept watch nearly all the day and in the evening at 11 pm the shooting party came off, the Captain first in his galley. We fired a rocket at 9 o'clock to show them where the ship was. Well, they came on all looking fearfully tired and bringing with them two buffaloes which we afterwards ate. The beef was much better though very tough, than the coast beef. We hoisted these animals in and the party all turned in. We learned from then the next day that Mr Nicholls and Nicholson had been the successful buffalo shooters. Roots had shot one but they did not bring it on board as it was too far away. They also, during the day, saw a couple of panthers, big ones too, and two wild boars with big tusks and the spoor of Hippopotami. Everybody, except Monckton and the paymaster [Mr. Aylen], were asleep in the hut when one of the panthers ran past and the paymaster, who was holding my gun in his hand, tried to fire it at him, but the cartridge was damp and so do not go off – and it was very fortunate

---

25 net

he did not, for if he had hit him with my small shot the panther would probably have turned and gone for him. All these animals were attracted to the spot by the smell of the entrails of these dead buffalo; one of the men saw the other panther drinking at a pool, so he turned like an idiot ran back to the camp as hard as he could and looked in a deadly faint when he arrived!!! Another man, our steward who was doing the cooking, came upon a wild boar suddenly, eating the entrails of a buffalo and he said he was a huge beast with big tusks, and he also was in a deadly funk and ran all the way back to the camp.

October 24 Cape Lopez

Raining hard all day. Number One went ashore with some kroomen and brought the beasts on board. I had buffalo heart and steak for lunch, very good. Steak rather tough, soup splendid. The buffaloes are just like huge cows with long curved horns. They are awfully thickset and their hide is ¼ of an inch thick.

October 26 Cape Lopez.

Left this jolly place for St Thomas Island and now I'm afraid I left off writing my diary for two weeks and only know the principal things that happened.

October 26

Arrived at St Thomas Island, a very pretty island something like Fernando Po, a few houses and a fort down by the water. We anchored in 7 fathoms in beautiful clear water – you could see the sandy bottom with shells on it distinctly and I was longing to bathe but there were too many sharks in the neighbourhood. We saluted the Portuguese flag with 21 guns and the fort returned our salute, then the Captain went ashore to pay his respects to the acting governor, Viscomte [*sic*] Pipeudi, or some such tally. Instead of seagulls large fish hawks fly about catching the fish. Every night it was very pretty to see all the fishing canoes away out at sea fishing with a large lighted torch in each. They stay out for about four hours and each canoe catches about 90 flying fish. One evening I counted 93 of these canoes. The natives on the island live almost entirely on fish, it is a Portuguese place.

October 28th

Left St Thomas for Quitta.

October 29th

Breakfasted with Capt Domvile, we had a bit of a yarn about nothing in particular and he was very nice.

November 1 Monday

Mr Prickett, Monckton and myself dined with the Captain and ate his last turkey, he was very nice and gave us a very fair dinner.

November 4 Thursday.

Arrived in Quitta – got three lots of mail, got some letters then went provisioning ship.

November 6 Saturday, Quitta.

Went ashore with Capt Domvile. Went to the castle and saw Captain Graves and Campbell. We went round with them and paid a visit to Chief Hickity. He wanted us to drink some nasty stuff, but we managed to get lemonade out of him! He gave Capt Domvile a turkey and one of his chiefs gave Captain D. a duck which he afterwards gave to me. Captain Graves told me that in the case of a row Chief Hickity could call 700 fighting men underneath his banner so that it was a good thing to keep friends with him, in case the governor wanted them. We came off in the surf boat in the evening without getting wet and I dined with the Captain. Monckton, who had gone ashore shooting with Nichols, had shot curlew only. Next day we left for Accra.

November 8 Monday Accra.

Arrived at Accra. Met HMS *Fram*. We found there had been an awful row, about 3000 natives were going to make a raid on the town and two kings were captured; they were prisoners on board the *Fram* with four or five of their wives, but however the natives changed their minds and did not make a noise. The *Fram* went up to Cape Coast Castle for our mails there.

November 10 Wednesday, Accra.

The Captain sent me ashore in the surf boat with dispatches for H E the

Governor at 8:30 pm. It took an hour to get ashore and it was intensely hot, then we did get onshore. I walked up to Bruce, the contractor and asked him to lend me his horse – they were the only ones in the place as I had to go to Christinberg with dispatches for H E [and] it was 3 miles or so – he said yes. Well, in due time, I saw some natives saddling the brute so I objected, being in uniform with a dirk on and asked for him to be put in the trap which he did, so I got on board my two wheel ship, whipped the engines up and went ahead full speed, nearly sticking on a rock and running aground on a sand bank. Well, he was not half such an awful brute as one would expect to see in such a place and belonging to a native.

So in about 25 minutes I drew into the Castle gates, throwing the reins to a native, I walked in and was shown into the Private Secretary's rooms. Capt Barrow gave me a drink and a couple of *Vanity Fairs* and he took my dispatches into the Governor, who was sick in bed so that I could not see him. They were over an hour making out an answer to the xxxx letter, during which time I was amusing myself in the billiards room.

At last Captain B brought me the answer and asked me to stay to breakfast which I would not do, so back I drove, and having returned the H & T to Bruce's and tipped his man, came down to the beach and waited for more than one hour and at last saw the cutter coming in, so I went out in the surf boat as there was a very bad surf. We shipped three huge seas and I got wet through to the skin, dispatches and all. When I got on board it was 1 o'clock so I shifted[26] and went and lunched with the captain who was greatly amused.

November 12 Friday – Accra.

Both homeward-bound mails came in: the *Biapa* and the *Congo*. Williams, who had changed his name to Bassett, went on board the former with all his gear to go home and join the *Bacchante* (lucky dog). He expected to get home in about 22 days. At 8.30 the Captain sent me on board the *Biapa* in the galley to find out what I could about Consul Hewitt going home and the row up the Bonny. I did not find out much. I

---

26 changed clothes

saw the new Calabar Agent and he told me a little about it which I wrote down. I saw old Williams and he took me around and showed me his cabin, which looked as if it were going to be very close and hot.

November 14. Accra.

Poor Cook, A.B., was awfully bad with fever. The *Fram*'s ship's company came on board to church.

Cook was one of the two men who broke their leave in Cape Lopez while ashore.

November 17, Wednesday, Accra.

Departed this life W. Cook, Able Seaman, aged 21 years, from fever. At 4 o'clock in the afternoon his body was placed in a coffin and put in a surf boat alongside. Walworth and myself went in the first cutter, Monckton and Nicholson going in the second cutter. We got onshore without getting wet because there was a very fair surf and we had good big surf boats. When we landed the men fell in, the coffin being put in a kind of cart drawn by the mourners, we went on slow march. We got to the cemetery in about 15 minutes and Nicholls went through the usual burial service then we lowered the coffin into the grave. We fired three volleys and then went back to the beach in about five minutes, got into the surf boats, got wet through going through the surf then into the cutters, got on board at 3 pm. At 7:30 pm the *Fram* came back without our mails.

November 19, 1880 Friday, Accra.

Expecting the mail to come in all day long. In the afternoon both watches were firing at a target with rifles. The Captain gave me some shots and I was very close to the target. A very hot day.

November 20 Saturday Accra.

Mail did not come in so came to the conclusion that she had gone down in the Bay of Biscay as it is very bad weather, with all my letters and clothes on board. I expected my things out by her.

Here endeth my diary. And now, darlings, I think I have written you a long Xmas letter. Mind you send it on to the darlings at Rockenham, and once more wishing the crowd of you a Merry Xmas and happy New Year.

HMS *Dido*, Fernando Po, November 28, 1880

My dear Uncle Godfrey,

Thanks very much for the tip you sent me, it will be very useful, as I want to buy a pair of boots. I can easily get it cashed. We have been having very good fun down on the south coast, we stayed at Cape Lopez for about a week where we did some fishing and I went buffalo hunting. Fernando Po is a very pretty place but very unhealthy. The island is about 25 miles long, about 15 broad and overgrown thickly with trees and dense jungle inhabited by creatures called boobies and monkeys. The peak here is nearly 11,000 feet high. The Cameroon Mountains which you see across the water in the distance are about 13,000 feet high.

After this we are going to Saint Paul de Loando, then to St Helena, then to Ascension and then, hurrah, the Cape of Good Hope. We will take about 3½ weeks going from Ascension to the Cape at sea, the whole time on salt fish. We are coaling ship tomorrow, which will be a very dirty work. The coal agent here is a man who has just finished his punishment for murder. He murdered a native up one of the rivers and was sent here for transportation. Now that he has finished his punishment the Spanish authorities will not allow him to leave the island without first having a lot of communications with headquarters about it. I am rather sorry for the man though I should say he deserves more than a short transportation.

I hope Auntie Eunice and cousin Ted and the others are quite well. Please give them all my best love. It is getting rather dark so I think I better stop, dear Uncle Godfrey.

HMS *Dido*, at Sea, 21st December.

The last letter that I was able to send you was from Fernando Po so I think you will have received it ages ago. Since then we have been down to St Pauls de Loando where there are no mails for England. This is the second time we have been to St Pauls. It is the best place on the coast, a Portuguese place. I went ashore once and played a little cricket and drank cocoa and played billiards at an hotel, and we bought one or two little things, but it is an awful bother because they do not understand either French or English. I went ashore in the Captain's galley on Saturday to bring the two English consuls off. They were saluted by seven guns.

On Sunday I went ashore again in the steam cutter to bring one of the consuls off. We had plenty of fresh eggs, milk and bread while we were there, which was a great blessing. I was taken very ill there with the diarrhea (I can't spell) and being very sick too. I must have eaten some poison so the doctor [Lt. Mitchell] put me on the sick list for the first time. I have had to stay in my hammock all Sunday. I take beastly medicine.

I was on the sick list for four days – the doctor took me off the list this morning and I'm now quite well again so don't be alarmed. One thing alone remains to be said is that I am as thin as ever. The coast has pulled me down awfully this time but thank goodness I have steered clear of fever. I hope the Cape will pull me together a bit. In a few days it will be Christmas Day, the second one I have spent away from my old home. I wish I was going to spend the next one at home. I shall feel much nearer to you at the Cape … We will pass St Helena about Tuesday next, so Xmas will be spent at sea, a funny Xmas too. No happenings or anything else. How happy you must all be at home, now, just about Christmas time. I am afraid I'm not able to send you any presents from this horrible out of the way place.

And now darlings goodbye, I shall add something more when we get to sending our letters – love and kisses to all the Irish darlings and everyone I hope you have a Merry Christmas. From me.

HMS *Dido*, St. Helena, 26th December 1880

Christmas Day has come and gone and I did not enjoy it one bit, we spent it at sea. We only arrived here late last night and came to anchor at 9 pm. Nearly every blue jacket in the ship was more or less drunk on Christmas day, and it was such a bother having to go forward to them to their messes because of course they all wanted you to go. One good thing was that they were not allowed to carry you round next morning. I had to get all my things ready myself because my servant simply had not recovered from the effects of his last night's dissipation. I suppose all you darlings spent a happy and merry Xmas which made up for mine.

Well, we are here, as I have said before this evening, and the Commodore we expected to find here was not here, he had gone down to the Cape at full speed because of the breaking out of the Boers and we expect to go down there too. We will probably first have to go up to Ascension Island to get our provisions and coal, but we do not know anything for certain yet as the Captain has not made known any orders. We have just had our monthly exams and I did much better than last time getting 693 marks. Last time I only got 512 so I have improved 181 marks in six months and exams were harder this time than last. I'm going to try and get over 1000 next time. We all did in the same order (8) Tawney about 936, (7) Nicholson about 800 (3) Faussett 693 and (4) Bruce 669.

My three months as assistant navigator is over on New Year's day. I'm rather glad because when we are at sea I have to turn out every morning at 5.30 and dress and relieve the deck. I don't care about that, especially when it is raining. I'm on deck by 6 and stay on deck keeping watch till 8.30. Then I go on deck at four in the afternoon and keep watch till eight, when I come down and have my dinner then usually turn in. We are all very well and now it is out lights, so darlings good night and Love to all. I think I shall have one ride here if I can get on shore.

December 29 Wednesday.

I went ashore early intending to ride round to Sandy Bay which is about 15 miles, but when I got ashore all the horses were engaged by the cricket party, Navy versus Army. They were going to play at Plantation House right on the top of the hill, distant 5 miles, so I was very much disappointed. I met Mr Knipe, the colonial secretary; he was very nice, took me into the Club, and we had a long yarn and then we went out and he tried to get me a horse, as he had lent his to a cricketer. So the only obtainable animal was the American Consul's buck jumper, which only a few days before had run away with the Consul and thrown him off, breaking one of his ribs and an arm. So there were two reasons: first, I did not know the Consul and last but by *no means least* I had never got on, or attempted to get up on, the back of a buck jumper, so I determined not to try the American Consul's. So I went and had lunch at the hotel and at 12 o'clock I started up the ladder, 699 steps, to walk up to Plantation House. Well I walked for about 2 miles and then, hurrah, I sighted a donkey, so I caught him and jumped upon his back and then sang out for two boys who were near, and they came and drove him on – but ¼ of a mile on a bareback donkey was enough for me, especially as he was very thin and had a backbone like a sharp knife, so off I got and walked. One of the boys procured an empty sack which was laid across the back of the ass. Then I got up and proceeded much more comfortably and galloped along until we came to the gate of Plantation House where I dismounted and dismissed the donkey and the boys with 18d, then I went to the edge of the cricket ground, but seeing a lot of ladies there I did not go in but went and took Monckton's horse out of the stables (I was going half with him) only I was paying 7d out of the 10d as I rode it. Well then, off I started for Sandy Bay. I had a beautiful ride, went through some lovely country and after losing my way several times and traversing over about 8 miles I got to the top of Sandy Bay. I went down some way, then I came up again and went off to Huts Gate where I had an A1 tea, and then I came back by some very pretty roads to Plantation House, where I found we had been beaten. So I delivered up Monckton his horse, and walked down, then came on board at about 8 o'clock. The next day, Thursday, I went to a dance given by the soldiers' officers at the Mess House where I had great fun. I enjoyed myself immensely, danced all the dances except four, and I am afraid I danced a great many with one partner, the prettiest girl in the room. I will not tell you everything or you might be amused! We came on board at about 5 o'clock.

7: The letters, 1881

January 1st Saturday

Started ashore at 9.30 with Bruce and found our horses waiting at the hotel, so we started for Longwood and soon arrived at Huts Gate where we found some of our Petty Officers, so we stood them a lot of beer and then we rode onto Sandy Bay and Plantation House, and then came back, had a good tea at Huts Gate, and then went on to Longwood Plain where we had a splendid gallop and I made my horse jump two or three small hedges. Then we came on down to the town where we had dinner and then we came on board.

Next day, Sunday

I was sent ashore in the gallery to bring off some ladies who were coming to church on board. I had great difficulty in getting them into the boat, because it was so rough and they were so nervous. After Church I went ashore and went and paid a visit to my fair partner and took her to Church, which I did not care about, being of a bashful nature.

Next day, Monday 3rd

The mail came in from the Cape and brought a lot of fierce news about the Boers fighting, so the Captain sent me ashore, being ADC[27] to the governor and port officer et cetera, to find out all news, and I brought off dispatches from HE, and then the mail went so I was unable to send any letters, which I was very sorry for. Well, the end of it was we were ordered down to the Cape immediately instead of right up to Ascension first, as we were going to do (study the map) so we had to remain two days longer to coal and provision.

On Tuesday the Harbour Regatta came off, our men pulled in two races but they did not win. It was a very small affair, and in the evening a dance, which lasted till five next morning, was given in honour of the *Dido* and the regatta, and I got leave to go and, needless to say, I found my fair friend there, with whom I had a very pleasant evening. Next day we about took 25 soldiers and a sergeant of the Royal Artillery on board, to take them to the Cape. We also took two officers, Lt Weigall, RA and Lt Donald Footer, Gordon Highlanders.

27 aide-de-camp

And now I must say goodbye, darlings, as I may not be able to finish this afterwards.

Table Bay, January 21, 1881

I am so sorry that my letter did not go last mail, but we met the mail at sea and as it was my watch I was unable to address all envelopes and post your letter. As it was, there were very few officers who got letters away at all. None of the official letters or the seamen's letters went. We took 13 days to get down here, nothing of much importance happened on the way. One day there was a tug of war between eight of the Royal Artillery mess and eight of our own blue jackets, and out of three tugs our blue jackets walked away with them twice. Then we, the Mids, and clerks used to play "Sling the Monkey" every night, and the next morning we found great blue marks all over our bodies. Simon will tell you what Sling the Monkey is.

Just when we got within about 30 miles of this place an awfully thick fog came on, so we had to stop and do nothing but whistle to prevent ships from running into us. Well, after about six hours the fog lifted a bit, so we came in and anchored for the first time in Table Bay, Cape Town. We saluted a French Admiral who returned the salute and we found a German man-of-war here too and a lot of merchant ships. Well, we got all the news about the fighting. There was not much except that the *Boadicea* had gone up to Natal and had landed 200 men who were on their way to the front (by 'going to the front', we mean going up to where the fighting with the Boer actually is). So Captain D. immediately telegraphed up to Natal and the Commodore to know what we were to do, and we have not yet got any answer.

The day after we got in (we got in here on the 18th) it blew an awfully hard South Easter. In the afternoon, we had both bower anchors down, we parted one cable at about four and parted the other at about six, so we had to steam out of the harbour and we got under the lee of a point of land called Green Point. We stayed there all the 20th steaming about just enough to keep off the rocks. The German ship was in the same condition as ourselves.

Today, 21st, the gale had abated somewhat, so we steamed to our anchorage and let go our sheet anchor. We were looking for our bower anchors all the morning, but now the wind has come up again nearly as strong as before so we have had to stop looking for the anchors. It is an awful bother because it takes so much time away from our chances of going to Natal. If we go to Natal, which we probably will as soon as we have coaled and provisioned, we will probably land about 106 men and the Gatling guns, and then we will march to the front and join the Commodore Naval Brigade.

If Captain D. goes, which he probably will, I am nearly certain to go as his ADC. If so, I shall see some fighting, won't that be splendid. I'm awfully excited at the idea of going. We march right up. We go by train to Pietermaritzburg, distance from Natal about 80 miles, then we have to march all the rest of the way to Newcastle. I don't know exactly how far that is, about 100 miles, then we shall have to wait for the troops, and then we march on to the relief of Pretoria on the way to which place we shall have a pitched battle and fight against 8000 Boers. They say that they pick out the officers more particularly, they are splendid shots and are all mounted. I don't know whether you know all the yarns or not but they are true.

I will tell you some of the yarns. They have killed all the officers of the 94th that were up there, barring Capt Lambert, I think it is, who survived, he and another officer were taken to the edge of the river and that they had to take their word that they would not fight against them any more, so they promised, then they were told they might swim across the river – go away! – so they jumped in. When they were quarter away over the river, the Boers began firing on them and killed the officer who was with the Captain, but he got away. They also took 50 of our men prisoner but, funnily, did not kill them only stripped them naked and then turned them into another State, and so they got down to Natal. Pretoria is 370 miles from Port Natal where we anchor and only 50 miles that can be done by train.

A telegram has just come from the Commodore and we are going to Natal immediately; we have got our anchors up. We have been invited to a dance at Wynberg but we cannot land as it is blowing too hard so we cannot go … One thing I forgot to tell you is that the Captain is very pleased with my exams this time. I have got 150 more marks in seamanship and 151 more marks in study than last time. He sent the quarterly report of all the officers home the other day to the government, and in the remarks he said I was also very neat in my dress, which is a great thing for him to say because he is perfect in his, and he also said that I was attentive to my duties on deck and was deserving of advancement; and for general conduct ashore and afloat he gave me *very good indeed*. I am still very good friends with the Captain, and I am most desirous of keeping so.

Thanks very much for your letter dated December 16. I have received none between that date and about those dated September 24; I presume though, from what you say in your letter of December 16, that you have received my box of curios. I hope you will not be disappointed, but I am afraid the jewellery I intended sending you is gone for ever unless we go back to the

Coast, as foolishly enough I did not get the money for the things when I sent them ashore because I was certain at the time we were going to Cape Coast Castle again in a month. My only chance now is if one of the gunboats goes there. I am so glad you have sent my watch out again. Thanks very much, it is waiting for me in Simon's Bay. I will be able to get it in two or three days.

January 23, 1881 Simon's Bay.

Thanks so much for your nice long letter, darling mother, it was so welcome I will answer it in a minute as soon as I have told you both the news. Well, we got our anchors up in wonderfully quick time and also got a telegraph from Natal telling us to go there with as much haste as possible, and saying that the Commodore had gone up to the front, so we have come round here to coal and provision..

Well, we are off to the war!!! We only took about eight hours steaming round here, we steamed about $8\frac{1}{2}$ kn.

Your letter that I'm going to answer is dated December 22, 1880, and you addressed it to the West Coast. The papers tell the news about us very badly. I think that the *Army and Navy Gazette* is best for news about the *Dido*. Carrie Walwyn sent me a newspaper cutting about decorations at Clifton Church, and I was very interested in the font decorations as it appears that you, mother, and the girls did it all. Miss C W sent me a pretty Xmas card and a funny purse. Thanks so much, darling mother, for the sweet card and such dear nice words.

Do you know that if we stay in Natal about this war for about a month we shall probably come home because the men will be very very likely to be more or less sick after landing and marching about and fighting. The native King I told you about at Accra, about November 18, was tried at Cape Coast Castle, and I believe a lot of his followers were hung but he did not see it.

I hope Sir Frederick will stay with you. If you can possibly manage it do send me out a photo of yourselves, just you two. I shall be contented with one of each of you two darlings. I'm afraid I cannot afford to have mine taken as well, if I could find time … I am *so glad* you have received my huge budget. I'm afraid you will feel sick before you get to the end … I shall miss no opportunity of writing to you now, so let me know what your dreams were about me on 6 November, Pappa and Mama. I don't remember anything unusual concerning me.

HMS *Dido* February 7, 1880 Port Natal

… Here we are again! I am not landed so don't be frightened, because I suppose you must have seen in the papers ages ago that the *Dido* have landed a detachment of the Naval Brigade and had taken two field guns up to the Front under Lieutenant Ogle and Sub Lt Monckton, both of the *Dido*. They landed 80 men from our ship and 20 from the *Boadicea* and they all went up under Lt Ogle's command. You know that about one month ago the *Boadicea* landed 130 men. There is every chance of our landing another field gun crew, 18 men. There's just a chance of Captain Domvile going up when Commodore Richards comes down, but I am not at all happy because there is only a very little chance of his taking me as ADC, because the Commodore did not take one.

Our Naval Brigade with Google and Monckton are now on the march to Newcastle and I hope they don't get shot. I should be very sorry; … We sent them a box of good things to eat the other day, which will be very welcome to them. This is a splendid thing for Monckton as he is sure to get his promotion over it, if he is not shot.

I did not receive any letters at all this last mail, I wonder why. Captain Domvile lives in the Commodore's house onshore there, doing his work, we hardly ever see him, he comes off about twice a week. I have not been ashore here yet because I have not got any money. As soon as I know that there is no chance of my going to the front I shall look forward to our going down to Simon's Bay, because this is a horrible place to live off, we are about 1½ miles from the shore, and we roll about fearfully and it blows awfully hard, so we get when you go ashore you go in a steam tug because you have to cross a large bar, very rough. If I go ashore at all it will chiefly be for the fun of crossing the bar. I believe it is a very poor place onshore, nothing to do except ride, which can't be done without money.

Oh! I would give anything, anything to land and go to the front and have some fighting. In any case now I shall get a medal, if they give one for this war, because the ship has been here and landed a detachment, so we shall all get medals, though really I don't care about a medal without fighting for it – don't you think it is very foolish giving medals to officers and men who have not been under fire?

I intend to take up the weekly papers of this place and cut out anything that I think may be of interest to you, noting whether the yarn be true or not as far as I know. They have put in such a lot of rot about us two ships. The paper reporter comes off to us and we give him a lot of foolish yarns, and next day we see us all in the papers in black and white!!! But the kid reporter is getting too cute now.

HMS *Tamar*, troopship, came in here on the fourth with the 97th on-board. What an awful state Ireland is in, indeed it is in much the same state as the Transvaal. Parnell and company being the ringleaders as they are, ought to be shot.

HMS *Dido* Natal, February 13th 1881

Thanks, dear Father thanks, very much for your most welcome Valentine, a valuable and most substantial one to me, also Mother for your nice letter, and darling sweet little Hilda's short and sweet note; tell Fermor to give her a good kiss from me. You asked me in your letter, mother dear, whether I received Uncle Godfrey's letter and tip, yes, I did, and I wrote and thanked him for it not more than two mails certainly after I received them. I keep an account of all letters I receive and send.

There is no more news about us sending any more men to the front. I was sent away in the cutter to a steamer for beef, vegetables et cetera yesterday, and the boat was nearly swamped, we all got wet through to the skin a hundred times. It has been blowing very hard for the last few days and the sea is very rough. I am at present undergoing a hardship, a punishment for a very slight offence indeed, given me by Mr Prickett, xxxxx, our first Lieutenant, after he had a bad breakfast. The punishment is having my leave stopped until further orders and keeping watch and watch for three days, which means I will draw up my punishment on a kind of form … and then, thank goodness, my mild punishment is over, making out of 72 hours, 36 hours watch on deck. After all this, won't you expect to see a wonderful sort of animal someday soon walk into your house. I have just now got through half of it. I have got one of Lett's diaries and have kept it since New Year's Day and I intend to carry on with it. It is very kind of uncle John for sending it to me … When my watch and watch is over I will thank him by letter.

We expect the Flying Squadron in here soon. I should like to go and look at the *Bacchante*. If I'm not allowed to be a mid on board her, I expect I shall be asked on board by Scott, the mid, an old chum of mine in the *Britannia*, dear old *Britannia*, the happiest days I have spent since being in the service. Now it is six, so on watch I go …

I have finished my 6 to 8 watch and have had my dinner, so I'm just going to scribble a little more. Captain Domvile, who has been living ashore all the time we have been anchored here, is coming off tomorrow to live on-board here again because the Commodore has come down again is therefore going to occupy the Admiralty house himself. We are rolling about awfully more than we ever did on the West Coast (I shudder as I write that down). If there really is an Ashanti war we shall probably go up to Cape Coast Castle but I sincerely hope and trust we won't. Not even the chance of fighting would induce me to go to that abominable place any more. I'm very disappointed at this place, and not being sent up to the front. Anyhow if medals are given, we will get one. The only place I want to be landed at now is "Old England".

Ogle and Monckton are getting on very well on the march, our little regiment of blue jackets are going up with the 15th Hussars and they have already caught up the 12th and 60th and the 97th is quickly catching them up so that there will be a small army by the time they reach Newcastle. One of our guns got stuck in a ditch on the way, the four oxen that were drawing it took charge and broke the shaft and upset the affair in a ditch, but that was nothing to our jovial blue jackets on the march. They actually gave a small entertainment to the 15th Hussars and some villagers belonging to a village they were passing through; they march about 16 miles a day and get wet through every night. Ogle and Monkton had to sleep on a waterproof sheet, underneath the wagon one night [when it was] raining hard because their team came to grief. They are both mounted on native horses, which require the frequent use of the spur. I am reading through Shakespeare now in my few spare hours, I mean minutes, so I'm getting quite political.

I hope you all enjoyed the pantomime. I wish I had been with you, it is a long time since I enjoyed myself.

February 14 Thursday

It is blowing to land so I am afraid that Captain D will not be able to come off today. I think I have exhausted my supply of news. A happy thought has struck me; perhaps you would like me to have my photograph taken. I will, as I can afford it now, and send Rockenham and yourselves some, but I think I shall have to wait till we go down to Simons Bay, because the photographer at Cape Town is better than the man here.

As soon as I get can get ashore here I intend to have a good ride. Horses ought to be pretty cheap, by and by, when the war is over, but I shall not spend anything else bar washing till I get to Simon's Town. Do you take in the *Army and Navy Gazette*, because it is much the best service paper to take in for information about ships; we used to take in the *United Service* but we have stopped it and now take in the *Army and Navy*. We do not know in the least how much longer we may have to stay here – certainly, I should think, till the war is over and our brigade comes down again. I hope our brigade don't get shot about much, because I like some of the men very much.

Do you know, I should like photos of some of you people, very much, Nora and Maud must be getting quite changed and dear little Hilda and Mary Bee I'm afraid are growing fast; when I'm home again they will be great huge girls, I suppose, and I won't be able to hop them about on my knee. I hope all are well at Severn House. Love to Aunt B. I wrote to Cousin Alfred the last mail. Give my very best love to all the darlings in Rockenham, I hope the wretches, Parnell, Dillon and co., will soon be transported or put out of the way somewhere. Love and kisses to yourselves, kindly to Miss Hartland.

HMS *Dido* Natal February 28th 1881

Many thanks, mother, for your letter and news, paper cuttings, and Nora and Hilda's letters, they were all very interesting, what fun you must be having.

Terrible news has come from the front today. You will have heard something about it in your papers, but I daresay I can tell you something you don't know. Anyhow 600 of our men went out to reconnoitre or something and 7,000 Boers attacked them and they were terribly cut up, only about 100 getting back to the camp, and General Colley was killed. And 34 men out of the 60 Naval Brigade engaged were killed, and three naval officers, a doctor and the gunnery Lieutenant of *Boadicea*, and Commander Romilly of *Boadicea* dangerously wounded. The *Dido*'s naval brigade, under our gunnery Lieutenant Ogle, were left in the camp to guard it, because they had only just arrived there and were therefore not quite recovered from the effects of their long march. So Lieutenant Ogle of "ours" is in command of the whole.

I would give anything to go up, I should like it next best in the world to going home and leaving this. Oh! How I wish I could think that was soon to be, it is not the length of time I'm away from home I mind so much, it is nothing compared to a more important reason. I am afraid we will have a long commission, because we won't leave this charming station for some time, and then we will have to work out our proper time on some other sweet station.

How very sad about the death of Monkton's aunt. I wrote to him to the front today. Thanks for the newspaper. I did not receive it!!! What a little swell Hilda must be with her writing and skating and all that sort of thing. Please give Captain Maxwell Heron my best love and tell him not to talk rot saying I'm lucky to be on the West Coast, and that no one ought to grumble who has not been in the Red Sea or East Indies; it makes me sick to talk about the West

Coast or any other coast. Thanks very much for the very nice story of the fight between our man o'war and three French ones, I liked it very much. What a quantity of snow you are having in England. Oh! How nice.

I went ashore the other day and went up to Durban, about 3 miles distant I did a lot of shopping and then came down to the Point and found the steam tug had already sailed so I had to stay onshore for the night. I got a bedroom at a very nice hotel and I had a long yarn with a gentleman, merchant kind of man, who had been a prisoner in the hands of the Boers, and they had treated him very kindly and then let him go. I wanted to have a few hours ride into the country but they wanted such unheard-of sums that I abandoned the idea.

I have not yet seen Maxwell, and at the present state of affairs I don't expect I will. What regiment is he in? I suppose the sixth Dragoons, as I heard he was in a cavalry regiment. I should like to see him awfully. And now my darlings goodbye. They say now that Captain Romilly is not killed, only dangerously wounded I'm very glad. [But] Colley's death is certain – poor Lady Colley, she lives at Pietermaritzburg and has only been married two years.

HMS *Dido* Natal March 6, 1881

We did not get one letter this time, the mail steamer left them behind at the Cape, so we will have to wait another week. Now the news: Captain Domvile has gone up to the front, to take command of the Naval Brigade in the place of poor Commander Romilly, who has just died of wounds received in the engagement at Laings Nek.

I am so sorry he has gone, and I am awfully disappointed not going myself; he told me he should have liked to take me, but he was not allowed to do so. It will be a very good thing for him, that is to say if he escapes being shot he will get a C.B. Have you heard this, that Joubert, the Commander of the Boer force, has 70 chosen men, the best shots, always near him and when he sees any leading officer he tells these 70 men to shoot him, so they all fire at him till he is shot and that is supposed to be the reason why nearly all the leading officers have been shot or wounded as yet. The Boers are given to telling the most awful falsehoods. They actually said that they only lost *one* man killed and five wounded at that engagement at Laings Nek, and they have stuck to it ever since, but some people say that they lost about 400. The *Boadicea* sent up 50 more men, who came out the other day and Lt Henderson who came out with them, and Lt Duncan of the *Boadicea* to the front. Do you know, it is an acknowledged fact at the front that the blue jackets do longer marches than the soldiers.

You never told me, mother, what regiment Maxwell Sheraton is in. I suppose it is the 6th Dragoons. I have not yet seen him. I have written to Uncle John and Miss Walwyn, so I expect I shall get shoals of letters from the latter for some time. How very sad General Colley being killed; Lady Colley is quite young and has only been married two years they say.

The *Dido* has lots of men at the front, as yet three killed, two dangerously wounded and two or three wounded, and I don't know how many are missing or prisoners; that is a good many, you know, out of 30 that left the ship. It makes me so wretched to think that there are men up there fighting away, risking their lives while I am down here doing comparatively nothing. I hope to see Sir Frederick Roberts – what fun if he is to take me up! I hope you asked him to.

The *Firebrand* has come here and I believe we and *Boadicea* are going down to Simon's Bay soon to meet the Flying Squadron and hold court martials, then when the war is over we will come up here again to collect our fighting Captain, officers and men. I'm thinking of going ashore tomorrow but I won't unless it is final. In case I do, I will finish this letter tonight, for I may not be off in time to post it. I cannot think of anything else to say. So goodbye. Give my best love to Darling Granny and the Fermor sisters.

March 7, 1881 Natal

[*To Father and Mother*] I went ashore today and did a little shopping and had a very fine ride round the country. I rode a very fresh mare, her name was Naughty Girl. We are going to sea tomorrow morning for target practice with our 64 pounder guns and are coming back in the evening.

There is a foolish rumour here that Sir H. Wood is a prisoner in the hands of the Boers, but no one believes it; also there is a lot of talk here about this armistice. I told a man on shore to send you a weekly paper, it tells the news of the week of this out of the way place. It was not printed when I was ashore, so I left your address. Next time I go ashore I shall call or leave my card on the Commodore; I forgot all about it today.

I wonder how soon Monckton will be in an engagement, he was not in the last at Laings Nek, perhaps it was better for him that he was not. I feel twice as well now as I was before I went ashore, as it is awful being cooped up on board for fortnights and sometimes for months at a time. I send you a newspaper cutting, an account of Captain Domvile departing for the front. I shall go and turn in now as I am rather tired after my day onshore …

PS I hope what I said about going ashore on the top of the page does not make you think that I am ill, because I'm quite well!!!

HMS *Dido*, Natal, March 9, 1881

I send you a letter we got from Monckton the other day giving an account of the engagement at Laings; I do not want it to go any further than you two and the Irish ones, as Monckton's people might hear of it. Monckton might be angry at my sending his letters home; anyhow I thought it might interest you as it was written by an eyewitness close to Laings Nek, so I send it. As Captain Domvile is up at the front now I always write my letters in his dining cabin as it is much nicer cooler and lighter than the wretched gunroom.

March 13th

I went ashore yesterday and walked up to Durban where I frotted[28] about for an hour, went to a sale of horses that was going on in a yard place, the auctioneer man making an awful row, and some of the most fearfully wretched horses I ever set eyes on being fetched out and sold. They fetched about £15 as a rule. I very soon left that affair and walked halfway down to the Point to Champions, the contractor; he had promised to lend me his horse to ride, so he had it saddled and I had a good gallop, right across the sands. The horse did not like it much as it was high tide and the breakers frightened him.

Coming off in the tug it was raining hailstones and very rough so we shipped any amount of big seas and also got wet through. I found a lot of letters waiting for me, letters from mother dated November 8 and 12th 1880, and Feb. 3rd and 10th 1881, they were all very interesting. I'm so very sorry that Mrs Miller of Brentry is dead. I hope Uncle Ernest is quite well again from his cold. I was sorry to hear that Billy Sheraton is finished with the Navy. I have not yet seen Maxwell Sheraton, and I'm afraid I won't either. I cannot help laughing at your anxiety about me and the war. I must say, though, that I am with father in wishing I was in the thick of it all!!! I hope that mad Gladstone does not come to terms of peace with the Boers (who are very brave). How fearful it would be.

I am so much obliged to Nora for her nice letters, I will write to her. I'm going to write to Monckton to tell him the little news, as I expect as he likes hearing civilised things where he is.

---

28 Victorian slang for 'masturbated' – but clearly in this case used figuratively, meaning 'wandered' or similar

March 14, 1881, Natal

[*To Aunt Edie*] Thanks so much for your two charming letters, dated October 7, 1880 and February 2, 1881. I may as well tell you to begin with, that which you already know, that is to say, but I'm not personally engaged in hand to hand conflict with the Boers. What fun you had in the sledge getting capsized et cetera. I hope next winter is the same as this. Mind you, send me an account of your visit to Dublin. I won't forget your message to Maxwell if I see him. I am so very glad that the last accounts I heard of Great Grandpa were favourable. Thanks very much for the *Irish Times*.

I have been ashore three times; the first time I did nothing worth mentioning, the second time I had more fun. I went to some livery stables here and asked for a saddle horse so I was taken to the stables, and the man said he had a nice fresh mare that had not been ridden lately and asked me if I would care to ride her, so I promptly said yes, so she was saddled, and I mounted. I asked what her name was and was told she was called the "Naughty Girl", so I thought she must be a beast, well I mounted, quite expecting her to commence a series of buckjumping, which is the favourite pastime of Cape Horses– well, I got away out of the stables, and onto the beach, which is all sand. I thought the sand would be the best thing to fall on but she did not commence any buckjumping at all, which I was rather glad of, she *only* shied at everything unusual she saw, and sometimes at things she did *not* see. When I found she was manageable I turned off the beach, right across country on her and had some fine gallops, she jumped 2 or 3 ditches which came my way, which made me very happy, and after three or four hours we went back again, the owner asking me if I and the mare had parted company at all during our travels (cheek).

Well the third and last time I went ashore was the other day. The tramway has just been opened here, so I got into a tram car (all same English) and we were driving along all right when the wretched thing went off the line [and] some old women who were inside commenced shrieking and yelling. After tremendous exertions on the part of the horses, driver and porter, the car got on the lines again, but I can assure you it gave a shock to my sensitive nerves. I mean the women shrieking did, and it must have confused the driver, for he did not wait at the next crossing – so in the middle of the road we met the other tram coming in the opposite direction, so after a good row between the two drivers as to which should go back they decided on shifting horses and people, which was done, and we proceeded on our journey. I don't think all the old ladies got into the car again, they were too frightened, so they went away, visibly trembling in every limb.

But after that little bit of excitement, I went to a man called Champion, a storekeeper, who had promised to lend me a horse he had, so I went and reminded him of his promise so he got the animal (big and black) saddled, informed me it was a very good saddle horse *only* it was given to stumbling, so I mounted and went off. I had intended to go to a hill along some roads, but hearing about his stumbling tricks and not deeming it wholly convenient to have to pay for his broken knees in case he came down on the road, I decided on taking him onto the sandy beach where he could not hurt, so I had one or two very feeble gallops which I did not enjoy, for about an hour and then I returned my most inferior steed to his good-natured master sweating a little.

Then I went up to Durban again and stopped for a short time to watch a horse sale that was going on. The auctioneer was making endeavours to be heard all over the Transvaal, and the horses, which were the most dreadful specimens of horseflesh were fetching from 9 to 18 guineas.

I soon left that and I came down and got on board the tug and came on board the ship, getting wet through, as it was raining, and being very rough, we dived through several big seas. We have lost a lot of our *Dido* own men, killed and wounded up at the front; of the three men who were killed in the second engagement at Laings Nek, two were hit in the forehead and the other in the chest, so all were killed facing the foe. Of the three wounded, one was wounded in the neck, the other through the back and the third through both hips.

It is very hot weather here now, I wish we would go down to Simon's Bay again.

HMS *Dido*, Natal 21 March 1881

Thanks very much for the diary. I received it last mail, and I received letters of the date of November 19, November 26, December 1, 1880 and February 7, 1881. Thanks very much for the beautiful Xmas cards and thanks very much, dear father, for the beautiful little boatswains pipe, I like it immensely. Major Parr wrote me a letter and sent it in it. I was unable to see him as he started for Pietermaritzburg some days ago.

I am so dreadfully sorry I am not at the front. If I can manage to have a talk with Sir Frederick Roberts, I shall not hesitate to ask him to take me, I hope he will, because it would be such glory. I am so glad you were pleased with the Captain's report of me to the Admiralty. I sent you two little scribbles, I hope they may help to amuse, I shall often send you some now.

I am awfully afraid we shall have started for Simon's Bay before Sir Frederick arrives here, we are only now waiting to see what is going to happen and whether we will be required any more. Six horses for Sir Frederick, value £100 each, arrived here the other day in the steamer *Melrose* from the Cape. We have been rolling fearfully since I last wrote to you, almost more than we ever did before, and it has been blowing very hard too.

It was 1.30 when I stopped writing and it is now eight, and a very sad accident has happened in that time. There is an awfully rough sea on the bar today and the steamer which came in this evening shipped a big sea while crossing the bar and two *Boadicea*'s men, the Commander, one servant and a krooman, were washed overboard and drowned. I'm sorry to say. Though, if they had been holding on they could not have been washed overboard. Capt Domvile arrived at Newcastle some days ago so by this time he will have reached camp at Mount Prospect.

I expect to find Monckton's box at Simon's Bay waiting for us, he has given me leave to take anything out, so I shall get my watch and other things. How are you getting on with the acrostics, have you won any prizes yet? I don't like these new Penny stamps a bit, I think those nice old red ones were much nicer. This letter is a very short one, but there is nothing to say here in this place, as I write every week.

HMS *Dido*, East London, March 26, 1881

Here we are you see, at another place, 260 miles from Natal, we left Natal at 5 o'clock last evening and are here at 2.30 this afternoon; smart work, was it not? We went 12½ knots for some part of the time. The reason for our coming down here is this; you know there is a telegraph cable from Natal to England and one or two other places, but not calling at Cape Town, and there is another cable from Natal to Cape Town, calling at this place. The cable from here to Natal is broken, so the authorities sent us down here with important dispatches that we were to telegraph onto Cape Town to stop Sir Frederick Roberts and the reinforcements from coming any further on account of the Peace – [a] *disgraceful* peace we all think it is out here.

I think we are going back to Natal tomorrow, we are going to leave our mail bag behind here in case we miss the mail at Natal. If we miss the mail at Natal I shall probably write again, so you will receive two letters at one and the same time. When we get back to Natal we shall be expecting daily to get our orders to go to Simon's Town because the Detached Squadron is there and we want to hold our court-martials with them.

My dear mother, you are much too sanguine in your idea that this ship is going home as soon as we get our men back, because it is highly improbable. I'm so sorry to disappoint you, I should not have said it was likely at all, but at the time I thought it was, so forgive me! I'm painting two very nice little pictures in Indian ink, my first try. I think they will be ready to send you next mail, you must not expect much as it is first try.

I must go and send my hammock down now but I will be back in a minute. I was very glad when we were here because on the very on the way down the ship was shaking awfully through our going so fast. This place is not nearly as big as Durban although it is a namesake of London. There is a very bad surf here too, a lifeboat (the same as English lifeboats) came off to us for our dispatches and it was manned by big white men. P is quite proud of taking the ship down here because he has command now that Capt D is at the front. Captain D will be very disappointed at not having any fighting.

HMS *Dido* Natal April 1, 1881

I hope you will not mind my writing this on "April Fools Day", but I will try not to humbug you as it is past 12 am.[29] I got a very interesting letter from Monckton to say he is at Newcastle with the remainder of the Naval Brigade, on their way down here, they are all very sorry (as are all of us) that there is to be no more fighting. The people ashore were burning effigies of Gladstone, Parnell and Bright the other day.

You see we have come back from East London where I last wrote from. We came along about 1 mile off shore all the way up, not as far in some places, and the scenery was simply lovely, at first it was high, then low land. The distance altogether is about 260 miles. We passed close to a river called St Johns River and the scenery is lovely, high cliffs on either side and long green plateaus halfway up the mountains. There is a signal station there and a fort, and they signalled to us they were "all well". Within a mile from the shore there no doubt were hundreds of animals, tigers and leopards, monkeys ad lib. When the land got lower we passed two Kaffir Kraals with some bullocks feeding on the turf; we also saw a herd of buffalo running about and a young buck or so; intensely interesting. One of our fellows is sending a sketch of East London with the *Dido* in front to the *Graphic*, so mind you look out for it and please send me a copy.

We buried that poor Krooman (that I told you had died) at sea as soon as

---

29 By which he will have meant 12 noon, unlike 21st-century parlance, in which 12 am usually means midnight.

we got out of East London. It is the first funeral I have seen at sea and it is a very melancholy affair, especially if the person buried was anyone you cared for. The Kroomen are very delicate. The name of the crewman that died was Jack Ropeyarn.

I'm so very sorry to hear that Lord Beaconsfield is so ill, I sincerely hope he gets no worse. The troopship *Euphrates* has arrived here with regiments, and it is a great disappointment to them all. I have written to Captain P. thanking him for bringing me out the parcel. He is at Pietermaritzburg, appointed DAAG.[30]

A white parrot or cockatoo flew off from the shore and perched itself on our rigging, so the signalman went up into the main top with some food which he placed on the top, and after about half an hour the bird came down into the top and began eating, so the signalmen got underneath and caught hold of the bird by the tail and it bit him awfully but he managed to bring it on deck. It is a very ugly bird with an enormous beak! I send you the two pictures I have drawn, it is my first shot with the Indian ink on a paintbrush so it is not good, but I like it very much so shall continue it.

My letter to Mxxx is the first he heard about his aunt's death, as his home letter went adrift somehow, so I am very glad I wrote to him twice, you know, and I gave him your one page, mother … We expect them all down here in about 10 days and then for Simon's Bay, which will be a week nearer home, for it takes seven days for our letters to come and go from here to Simon's Bay. It is 8.30 and I have no more to say, as it is my morning watch, which means turning out at four, so I will bid you a good night.

April 4, 1881 Natal.

Here we are again; thanks for your letter, mother, dated March 8. Monckton's box came out, and according to his instructions I unpacked them and had his guns stowed in his chest, and I was happy at finding one or two things for myself, my watch, silk suit [?], books, clothing et cetera! I'm so glad I have the watch again; it is very useful. Thanks so much to darling little Hilda and Baby for their letters, I will answer them next mail, and also many thanks for Nora's. What a dreadful affair the Emanuel church catching fire. I suppose Sir Fred is very sorry at not having the chance of still more distinguishing himself, though I should hardly think that the governorship of this place was a good enough billet for him.

On Saturday last I went ashore with Bruce; a lot of soldiers and officers

---

30 Deputy Assistant Adjutant General

were in the tug coming ashore. They came out in the *Euphrates*, you know. Well, I brought any amount of curiosities. I bought an assegai and a couple of knobkerries and a lot of minor curios which I will send you when I next get the chance. The kaffirs are not allowed to carry knobkerries about with them through the town unless they have a pass. The kaffirs go about with their ears [and] noses [and] hair, or rather wool, stuffed full of all sorts of things, fancy snuff boxes etc. They are very fond of snuff, so next time I go ashore I shall see if I cannot buy some of their funny things out of their noses etc.

Coming off in the tug, the bar was rather rough, and as there were lot of Army and Navy officers on board, all the army officers had to go down below, so that they should not be washed overboard, and only the Navy officers were allowed to breathe the fresh air on deck. We went to the *Euphrates* first, to ship their officers, and one of the lieutenants asked me and the other officers to come on board, so we went and looked around got into conversation with a clergyman, who was on a pleasure trip, the brother of Captain Hands of the *Euphrates*. We had a long yarn, he was very nice and I asked him to come on board here and see me the next day but he was unable to come, no boats being able to come on account of the rough sea.

There is a yarn that the *Bacchante* is coming round here. I don't think it is likely though. I shall send you a knobkerry, Father, and it will do for a walking stick in the country, they are splendid things, you could kill a cow with them very easily. The Kaffirs use them in war, it would be a splendid thing for you to carry, Father, in our election row or a home-rule or land agitation affairs. I shall use mine for slaying mad dogs, snakes and such like animals that humbug you in this part of the world. I hope I see Maxwell before either his regiment or my ship leave here.

Those silk things that Aunt Emy sent me will be most useful, I can wear them at night because my nightshirt gets wet through perspiration and the silk would be much cooler, we call them pyjamas out here. Dear little Scamp, our terrier, has got a new collar, he is a great friend of mine. I'm going to have my nightly cup of cocoa in a minute when I have finished this letter. I'm looking forward to getting my things as I want some of them very much, I will get them we get down to the Cape. Lady C is going home shortly.

HMS *Dido* April 10, 1881 Natal

Many thanks for letters from all. I have not yet got the things for Monckton, which were to be addressed to me, I expect they will be at Simon's Bay. We expect to go to Delagoa Bay soon – our new British possession, you know – to hoist the British Flag there; it is a very unhealthy place, I believe. I send you a sketch of the death of General Colley from my imagination. I hope it will amuse you.

I went ashore the other day again and bought one or two things. On Thursday I was asked by the Reverend Hands to lunch on board the *Euphrates*. He is a brother of the captain, so I went and lunched and went all over the ship afterwards, she is a magnificent ship, huge compared to this. Hands is a very nice fellow indeed.

There was a railway accident ashore here the other day, I went and looked at the scene, the only mishap was the breaking of a leg of the engine driver; it was a goods train and the engine and first truck had completely turned over. We expect Captain D. and the men down in about a week's time. I wonder who has won this time in the Oxford and Cambridge boat race? I have made one or two bets on Oxford.

I caught a lot of fish the last two nights, fishing in the first and middle watches. The first night I caught eight or nine, the biggest weighing about half a pound and the second night I caught 11, biggest ¼ pound, they are splendid eating. I don't remember what they are called out here. I wore my silk pyjamas last night for the first time, and they are delicious, so nice and cool. We have broken all our lamp chimneys, so as we cannot get any ashore here; we have to steal ships candles and shove them in saucers and bottles. I am the only member that sports a candlestick; the best dodge at present is a candlestick in a ginger beer bottle and the bottle suspended by wire to the bar going overhead. I bought a big drawing book ashore and I'm going to draw a picture of some sort on each page, and when it is full I will send to you. I have nearly finished one already and done it in Indian ink.

The two troop ships *Euphrates* and *Tamar* went away yesterday, the former bound for Ceylon with the 102nd Regiment and the latter bound for Merry England with the widows and children of killed soldiers. I'm so very glad I have got my watch again; it is very useful especially as I take the times for all evolutions[31] … I have kept my diary from 1 January omitting only a very few days, a feat which I have never been able to accomplish before.

I cannot find anything more to say, for the life of me. Cockroaches are horribly numerous, and every so often three or four are running about in my chest when I open it. I always kill them when I can. Rats are not as numerous, as Scamp kills too many and frightens a great many more. There are also three or four cats which, if they do not kill rats, at least at all events they frighten them.

---

31 drills to practise routine procedures

HMS Dido Natal April 16th

One letter from you this mail … The other day all the midshipmen were sent away in boats sailing, and I was sent to sail the gig, so I sailed her and I went too far away – and as there was a very strong tidal tug I was drawn down right onto the bar, which was very bad at the time, and I only saved the boat from being swamped, capsized and all hands drowned, by the skin of my teeth. The first lieutenant was in an awful funk, he sent the bosun away in another boat after me and there was a tremendous excitement, but I did not mind a bit, rather a joke than otherwise, we at last were managed to save ourselves from going on the bar and we went on board again. The First Lieutenant gave me the most awful rowing, saying that he had not seen such a dangerous thing since he had been in the ship, that I was endangering the life of my crew of four men, the boat and myself, but it is all right now and waters are about as smooth as ever.

The Naval Brigade are down here today, but as it was blowing they are not coming off until Monday.

April 17

The other day, it being Good Friday, a man (reporter for one of the Natal papers) came aboard the ship to see her and to take some washing for some of the officers. Well, not knowing the strict discipline of one of Her Majesties [*sic*] Ships of War and being a little screwed, he came over the side with a bottle of grog showing in one of his coat pockets. Well, the First Lieutenant happened to see this so he made a prisoner of him at once, with a corporal over him – rather amusing, I expect he rather cursed his visit to the ship. In the afternoon, it being my watch, when he was brought aft onto the quarterdeck I had to see him and he requested that he might be allowed to go underneath the forecastle as he was very cold, and indeed the poor brute looked miserable so I allowed it; I expect we'll see some fearful stories about the ship in tomorrow's papers. He was sent ashore in the evening steamer.

The wounded men have not come down with the rest of the brigade and tomorrow at 2:00 pm Commodore Richards CB ADC is going to inspect them, numbering in all about 160 men. Then they are going to march from Durban to the Point (2½ miles) with the *Boadicea*'s band playing, and there they embark, and come on board their respective ships. There are about 80 to come to us, one wounded, one still at Newcastle. HMS *Boadicea* is going down to Simon's Bay this day week, where she remains two weeks, and then up the

West Coast she goes, poor thing! I don't know how much longer we have got to stay here – one and ½ months I expect – then we go to Simon's Bay. The gun room looks very nice [and] now that it is finished we are thinking how to arrange the assegais. I shall take mine home with me soon, *I hope*. I have also purchased a Zulu drape, not a very large piece of clothing and made out of the skin and tails of animals. I have been arranging my photos all today in my book. I'm looking forward getting to Simon's Bay so that I can go up to Cape Town and have my photo taken to send you. I've made up what I think is a beautiful piece of poetry about Heppington!

April 18, 1881

The Naval Brigade has not come off owing to bad weather, so we expect them tomorrow. I have just written a letter to Fermor. There was a grand parade onshore today; the Naval Brigade from the two ships and Commodore Richards CB ADC inspected them. Capt Domvile was mounted on a very nice horse.

A fellow was just getting a paper out of the locker overhead when a beast of a cockroach fell down and landed on my right ear. There are hundreds of them in the gun room. Brown lost his dirk overboard the other day, getting into his boat; I expect he will leave us soon and go back to the *Boadicea* again. It will be a great bother as it will put us in three watches again.

I have only missed writing to you once since we have been in this place, that is now about three months. I hope you received all my letters. I was arranging my photos in my book all yesterday.

* * *

The transcription ends with that letter, although his diaries continue. Why the transcriptions ended is, however, a mystery.

Postscript

This is a very rare record of the late Victorian naval era and the family relationships brought to life through the eyes of a teenager's letters home.

Bryan Godfrey-Faussett was typical of many young men of the period – and indeed of those who went to sea in the many decades to follow. That his letters have survived is a rarity, and opens a window into the Victorian navy.

His formative experiences both afloat and ashore brought him maturity earlier than his contemporaries and was a foundation for his future – as it was to me, many years later.

Primary sources

Churchill College Archives Centre
The papers of Sir Bryan Godfrey-Faussett:
BGGF 1/5
BGGF 1/6
BGGF 1/7
BGGF 1/8
BGGF 1/9
BGGF 1/10
BGGF 1/11
BGGF 1/12

United Kingdom Hydrographic Office Archive Department
Africa Pilot Volume 1 1874
Africa Pilot Volume 2 1874
Africa Pilot Volume 3 1874.
Admiralty Chart No. 591 Africa, Sheet 2: From the River Gambia to Cape Lopez and Anno Bom, 1812,1826 & 1839,1846.
Admiralty Chart No. 604: The West Coast of Africa from Banda Point to St. Paul de Loando 1825.

Secondary sources

Churchill Archive Centre: *Sir Bryan Godfrey Godfrey-Faussett, Knight, Captain, 1863–1945*. Cambridge, 2005.
Coad, Jonathan: *Support for the Fleet: Architectural Engineering of the Royal Navy's Bases 1700–1914*. English Heritage, Swindon, 2013.
Hall, Basil, Captain, RN: *The Logbook of a Midshipman*. Blackie & Sons, London, 1901.
Johnson-Allen, John: *'Rosy' Wemyss, Admiral of the Fleet: The Man Who Created Armistice Day*. Whittles Publishing, Dunbeath, 2021.
Padfield, Peter: *The Victorian and Edwardian Navy*. Pimlico, London, 1981.
Scott, Sir Percy, Admiral, RN: *Fifty Years in the Royal Navy*. John Murray, London, 1919.
Wells, John, Captain, RN: *The Royal Navy: An Illustrated Social History 1870–1982*. Alan Sutton Publishing, Stroud, 1994.